An Introduction to Ancient Mesopotamian Religion

Tammi J. Schneider

WILLIAM B. EERDMANS PUBLISHING COMPANY

GRAND RAPIDS, MICHIGAN / CAMBRIDGE, U.K.

Published 2011 by
Wm. B. Eerdmans Publishing Co.
2140 Oak Industrial Drive N.E., Grand Rapids, Michigan 49505 /
P.O. Box 163, Cambridge CB3 9PU U.K.

Printed in the United States of America

17 16 15 14 13 12 11   7 6 5 4 3 2 1

Library of Congress Cataloging-in-Publication Data

Schneider, Tammi J. (Tammi Joy), 1962-
    An introduction to ancient Mesopotamian religion / Tammi J. Schneider.
        p.   cm.
    Includes bibliographical references (p.   ).
    ISBN 978-0-8028-2959-7 (pbk.: alk. paper)
    1. Iraq — Religion.   I. Title.

BL2350.I7S36   2011
299'.21 — dc22

                                                    2011009324

www.eerdmans.com

AN INTRODUCTION TO ANCIENT
MESOPOTAMIAN RELIGION

With my greatest thanks
To my mentor
James D. Muhly

Contents

Acknowledgments

As a single-authored volume, all the problems, mistakes, and flaws fall completely upon the author. Despite that, there are many who deserve this author's greatest thanks and appreciation.

Allen Myers originally brought the idea of this book to me. I appreciate his suggestion that I was able to carry out such a complicated project, especially since I enjoyed researching this so much. The editors at Eerdmans have been helpful and polite throughout the whole process.

My students at Claremont Graduate University and Claremont School of Theology bore the brunt of figuring out how to approach the topic and what to do with a number of issues. Their commitment to their own research and enthusiasm for their topics, especially the Mesopotamian deity they were assigned as their project (even surprising me on the last day of class dressed as their deity with offerings to themselves), brought the topic to life.

As always, my family deserves my thanks. My mother is my rock. My family, immediate and extended, is always excited about whatever I am doing. My husband, Farooq Hamid, and my daughters, Kalilah and Sarah, ground me.

I am also lucky to have a great mentor, James D. Muhly. He accepted me as a student, trained me, and still sends me articles with little sticky notes attached. In recent years, I have become part of his family, possibly his greatest gift to me of all.

Abbreviations

ABD	*Anchor Bible Dictionary,* ed. David N. Freedman
ANET	*Ancient Near Eastern Texts Relating to the Old Testament,* ed. James B. Pritchard
AnOr	Analecta orientalia
AOAT	Alter Orient und Altes Testament
APSP	*American Philosophical Society Proceedings*
AS	Assyriological Studies
Bib	*Biblica*
CAD	*The Assyrian Dictionary of the Oriental Institute of the University of Chicago*
CANE	*Civilizations of the Ancient Near East,* ed. Jack M. Sasson
CBQMS	Catholic Biblical Quarterly Monograph Series
COS	*The Context of Scripture,* ed. William W. Hallo
HSS	Harvard Semitic Studies
JCS	*Journal of Cuneiform Studies*
JESHO	*Journal of the Economic and Social History of the Orient*
JNES	*Journal of Near Eastern Studies*
OEANE	*The Oxford Encyclopedia of Archaeology in the Near East,* ed. Eric Meyers
OIP	Oriental Institute Publication
OLA	Orientalia lovaniensia analecta
Or	*Orientalia*
PIHANS	Publications de l'Institut Historique et Archéologique Néerlandais à Stamboul

RA	*Revue d'assyriologie et d'archéologie orientale*
SAA	State Archives of Assyria
SAACT	State Archives of Assyria Cuneiform Texts
SAOC	Studies in Ancient Oriental Civilization
SBLSymS	Society of Biblical Literature Symposium Series
SBLWAW	Society of Biblical Literature Writings from the Ancient World
TCS	Texts from Cuneiform Sources
YNER	Yale Near Eastern Researches
ZA	*Zeitschrift für Assyriologie*

CHAPTER 1

Introduction

The world of ancient Mesopotamia was filled with a number of deities whose responsibilities and powers shifted over time and place, similar to the political reality of the region. Contrasting and yet paralleling these phenomena is that, like other realms of ancient Mesopotamian civilization, many fundamental components of ancient Mesopotamian Religion continued unchanged for centuries in the region. The basic operating premise for the ancient Mesopotamians throughout all periods of their history is that humans were created and placed on earth so the gods did not have to work. Each deity controlled different elements of the world order, so no one god had full control, and which deity was in charge fluctuated over time and place.

Gaining a clear handle of what constituted ancient Mesopotamian religion is complicated by two principles governing its modern study: that a "Mesopotamian Religion" should not be written,[1] and that there is a Mesopotamian "stream of tradition"[2] beginning as early as the third mil-

-----

1. Oppenheim, *Ancient Mesopotamia*. Oppenheim suggests the reasons for not writing a Mesopotamian Religion: "the nature of the available evidence and the problem of comprehension across the barriers of conceptual conditioning" (172); both issues continue to exist. Despite his cry not to write such a treatise, to some extent in the pages included under this heading, he proceeds to do so. The power of Oppenheim's statement on the field is revealed in a recent study of Mesopotamian religion where Oppenheim's claim is invoked in a chapter entitled "The Sources: What We Can Expect from Them." See Bottéro, *Religion in Ancient Mesopotamia*, 26.

2. Oppenheim defines this loosely as "the corpus of literary texts maintained, con-

lennium B.C.E. and continuing through to the first.[3] Both issues determine how one writes about the religion and the boundaries of Mesopotamia geographically and temporally.

Even A. Leo Oppenheim, despite cries to the contrary, wrote about Religion in Mesopotamia. Such can be done, as long as one is careful about what the data can and cannot support. As Piotr Michalowski has noted, "the challenge that lies before us is to confront the illusion of cultural unity implied by the 'stream of tradition' with the historically documented discontinuities in Mesopotamian social and political history."[4] As such, the title of this book, while simple, is relevant to what will and will not be covered in the following volume. I will begin by going over each element of the title because the definition of the different parts lays the groundwork for what to expect in the following text. With the ground rules established, I will review the approach to the project.

An: While this may appear an obvious inclusion to the title, the emphasis here is that the author recognizes this is not the final say on the topic but one of many approaches. It highlights that other approaches to the topic exist and there are certain to be more. This volume happens to be one particular option.

Introduction: In this context, the definition of "Introduction" meant is "a preliminary guide or text."[5] This volume is not intended to be the final scholarly word on any issue, but rather a preliminary guide for students of the ancient world. I will attempt to introduce the student to the various concepts and provide general background information so the reader can situate the data in its context. Since ancient Mesopotamia is somewhat foreign to most students of religion and the ancient world, one goal is to introduce what issues are even relevant to its study — explaining, for example, why this volume contains a section on the history of the area.

Ancient: This term carries different chronological implications depending on where and how it is used. Thus, "ancient history" is defined as

---

trolled, and carefully kept alive by a tradition served by successive generations of learned and well-trained scribes"; *Ancient Mesopotamia*, 13.

3. "Ever since Jacobsen's penetrating study of the Sumerian king list, it has been clear that unity and linearity were something the Mesopotamians foisted onto their past, rather than qualities which grew from it"; Lieberman, "Nippur: City of Decisions," 128.

4. Michalowski, "Sailing to Babylon, Reading the Dark Side of the Moon," 192.

5. *Webster's New World Dictionary: Second Collegiate Edition* (1986), 739.

"history from the beginning of recorded events to the end of the Roman Empire in the West in 476 A.D.," but "ancient" is "of times long past; belonging to the early history of the world, esp. before the end of the Western Roman Empire."[6] Depending on context, the impact of ancient Greece and Rome on the use and understanding of "ancient" is more significant than that of Mesopotamia. The bulk of the periods considered in this volume predate Rome completely.

A standard treatment of "ancient" with regard to Mesopotamia is to begin somewhere around the origins of writing, just before the beginning of the third millennium B.C.E. and ending with the conquest of Alexander the Great and/or the death of Darius III in 330.[7] Another ending point for the discussion of "ancient" Mesopotamia is the conquest of Babylon by Cyrus of Persia.[8] The reason for the conflict in end dates concerns how one defines the parameters of the study. Cyrus was welcomed by the citizens of Babylon, and, on the surface, life in Babylonia does not appear to have changed significantly, at least initially. The reason for ending at this point, however, is that from this moment, and for the next few centuries, Mesopotamian cities are ruled by the nonnative rulers whose seat of government is outside of Mesopotamia.[9]

The beginning point is separated from the Prehistoric period because of the introduction of writing. This also coincides in general with the beginning of the Bronze Age in the ancient Near East and the establishment of fully urban, relatively stable, developed societies.[10] At the ending point, the

6. *Webster's New World Dictionary*, 51.

7. The entry on "Mesopotamia" in *OEANE* consists of three separate articles, one of which is "Ancient Mesopotamia" (Hans J. Nissen, 479-84); following the article on "Prehistoric Mesopotamia" (Nissen, 476-79), it begins with the opening of the third millennium and ends with the death of Darius III, while the next article, "Mesopotamia from the Death of Alexander to the Rise of Islam" (St. John Simpson, 484-87), begins with the death of Darius III and the conquest of Alexander. Other histories of the area use a similar historical breakdown, including Kuhrt, *The Ancient Near East c. 3000-330 B.C.*; and Van de Mieroop, *A History of the Ancient Near East ca. 3000-323*.

8. Roux, *Ancient Iraq*, includes a final chapter entitled "Death of a Civilization," where he explains why those periods are not relevant and thus is a good example of the phenomenon.

9 Note that there are periods of ancient Mesopotamian history where "foreign" rulers dominate Mesopotamian politics, but they rule from within Mesopotamia.

10. Kuhrt, *The Ancient Near East c. 3000-330 B.C.*, 1:9.

conquest of the ancient Near East by Alexander the Great and the death of Darius III, the last Persian king, the political change or the Hellenization of the region was greater than earlier invasions. Also at issue is this volume's focus on the religion of Mesopotamia.[11] The Persians were centered outside Mesopotamia, in what is modern Iran, and the Persians had a different religious system. Accordingly, the conquest of Babylon by Cyrus will mark the end date for this overview of Mesopotamian religion. This does not mean ancient Mesopotamian religion ended on that date, but it was no longer the state religion of a self-governing body. This point then inaugurates the beginning of something new, and thus the end of our inquiry.

Mesopotamian: This term governs the parameters of the geographical area considered. In general, Mesopotamia is considered to be the area between the Tigris and Euphrates rivers. The territory corresponds primarily with the modern country of Iraq. The precise boundaries have varied throughout history, especially concerning the northwestern limits of the region. The eastern end of the area is the Persian Gulf, where both rivers end. The western boundary is more fluid, because technically there are areas between the rivers up to the sources of each, located in what is modern Turkey.

A major factor is that the rivers are more spread apart at their origins than at their ends, and the cultural connection of the areas west and north of Mari are less culturally tied to the rest of Mesopotamia. As with many other issues surrounding ancient Mesopotamia, which areas are central to Mesopotamia as opposed to peripheral changes over time. Thus, in the third millennium, the territory later occupied by the Assyrians is rather peripheral to Mesopotamian culture, whereas most scholars consider it to be within the region in the second and first millennia. It is likely that at the height of Assyria's power there were some, especially those living in Babylon, who also might have argued against considering Assyria as part of the Mesopotamian stream of tradition.

For the sake of this study, the western boundary of Mesopotamia will be the modern border between Iraq and Syria, and the subtleties of this border will be addressed for specific time periods and issues as is relevant. I admit that this is rather arbitrary; however, based on recent archaeological excavations conducted in Syria scholars have learned that from the third millennium B.C.E. through the first, there were cultural centers with their

---

11. To be defined below.

own character fairly distinct from that of Mesopotamia proper. Furthermore, because of the proximity of these areas to other ancient Near Eastern groups and influences, both the history and the culture of these areas differ enough from Mesopotamia to fall outside the confines of this treatment.

Religion: This element may be the most difficult to describe. The parameters of what constitutes religion have changed significantly in the last fifty years, especially since Oppenheim wrote.[12] Western scholarship has been heavily influenced by Christianity, and the view of what "counts" as religion and what does not often was influenced more by how any set of belief systems and practices correlated to those espoused by Christianity at the time and within a particular denomination of Christianity.[13] Christianity has a significant focus on personal belief and private devotion, elements almost completely absent from the records in Mesopotamia. Gary Beckman's title for his article on religion in the ancient Near East, "How Religion Was Done," neatly represents the shift to a newer approach to studying and treating religion, especially in the ancient world. His definition of religion, with a slight modification, will stand as a working definition for this volume:

> Religion here is the totality of beliefs and practices within a particular society that structure the relationship of men and women to [each other and] to the unseen but ever-present beings and powers with whom they share their world.[14]

Design of This Volume

Such a new working definition of religion does not alleviate all of the pitfalls Oppenheim noted, but it does allow the modern scholar of the ancient world to approach the study of religion through the remains left behind. This is the approach attempted in this volume. The book is designed to introduce students to the categories of data available and to the practices described in ancient documents and how they can be evaluated. Chapter 2 explains the extant data, with a bit of background as to how they

12. Oppenheim, *Ancient Mesopotamia.*
13. Smith, "Religion, Religions, Religious," 269-84.
14. Beckman, "How Religion Was Done," 366. My slight addition is in brackets.

were discovered and treated since their discovery. One premise behind this evaluation is that Mesopotamian religion changed over time — what Mesopotamian religion was differed throughout the various historical periods. For this reason, a brief overview of ancient Mesopotamian history is provided (ch. 3), focusing not as much on the concerns of a historian but on the information that would impact and act as a probable background for a change in the religious practices and/or beliefs in any given period.

Having established the general background, the investigation will turn to a study of the types of data available. One of the largest data sets concerning Mesopotamian views of the world is their myths, and these will be the starting point (ch. 4). Some of the major players in the mythological texts are the gods, so we will next survey who the gods were, how they changed, and their relationship to the Mesopotamians (ch. 5). Note that the myths are not the only source of information left behind about their deities, so other sources addressing the gods, both textual and visual, will be considered. Many of the religious structures from the ancient world center upon the gods, and an examination of those will follow (ch. 6). Priests officiated at the temples, but there were numerous other religious personnel working in and outside of the temples (ch. 7). Also, people with other titles that in the modern world are not considered "religious personnel," but must be considered so for the ancient world, will be investigated as a separate category. What happened in the temples and the actions of the priests were recorded, and those texts have been discovered (ch. 8). These provide a great deal of information concerning what, as Beckman notes, was "done" (ch. 9). Finally, the ancient Mesopotamian kings shared — or suggested that such was the case — a special relationship with their deities. Since the role of the kings was fundamental in the religious construction of the state, the relationship of the kings and the deities will be considered separately (ch. 10).

Please do note what is not in this volume. This volume is intended to be an introduction to the topic and thus does not provide a full examination, including an exhaustive bibliography of all of the scholarly literature. At the same time, it is frustrating if one reads about an interesting topic when the source is not cited at all, making it difficult to trace the author's tracks. I have tried to include enough footnotes and bibliography so that students can trace my steps and more fully investigate a topic without overwhelming others who are not interested in detailed notes. I have also assumed a primarily English-speaking audience and have included bibliography primarily in English.

Babylon (ca. 604-561 B.C.E.), with the Euphrates, Esagila (left), and the Marduk temple (right) in the foreground. *(Painting by M. Bardin, following E. Unger's reconstruction) (Courtesy of the Oriental Institute, University of Chicago)*

It is also not the goal of this introduction to provide a full analysis of every component of ancient Mesopotamian religion, since this could not be accomplished in one volume. I have tried to provide some general conclusions and parameters about the various components of ancient Mesopotamian religion and to then offer a few specific examples to show how that manifests itself and, usually, how that concept changed over time, often with some discussion as to why.

This is also not a volume of comparative ancient religion or comparative religion in general. People have some very set ideas about religion, especially their own. I have learned in teaching that for many students, it is easier to address concepts in religion from the ancient world because the adherents to those religions no longer exist and so there is no fear that by examining certain concepts someone will be offended. It is with this in mind that I have not added comments about how various concepts were then picked up by other religious groups or how similar some of these ideas may be to other religions. I confess that often I made those connections but have decided to allow the reader of this work to draw her or his own conclusions.

My goal was to provide a fair overview of ancient Mesopotamian religion and each of the various components that I think constitute our modern study of the subject. In the process it has become clear that trying to find the middle of the road in scholarship and summarize topics upon which large research volumes are written is no small task. The fields in Mesopotamian studies in general are small in terms of the number of scholars competent in the necessary languages to do solid primary research in the field, excavate in the areas covered, and become fluent in the art of the region, and yet vast when considering the large amount of data in ancient languages excavated in only the last hundred and fifty years. Thus, I am certain that inadvertently I have simplified complex topics, and skipped texts that may suggest a slightly different angle on a problem and for that I apologize in advance.

Ancient Mesopotamia, as Oppenheim noted, is far away both temporally and geographically.[15] Because the Mesopotamians seldom recorded what they thought, the goal of this volume is not to analyze how they felt about their gods or the universe but rather to investigate what they *did* based on the information they left behind to inform us of their world. This is, by definition, an incomplete picture but a fascinating one nonetheless.

15. Oppenheim, *Ancient Mesopotamia*, 172.

CHAPTER 2

Tools for the Study of
Ancient Mesopotamian Religion

The tools available for the study of religion in ancient Mesopotamia are based, to a large extent, on one's interpretation of what religion is. Using the older paradigm where religion focuses on people's beliefs, texts are the only serious tool available for understanding ancient religion. With the slightly broader definition used here, artifacts and architecture play a larger role. As such, knowing what tools are available to try to recover any sense of ancient Mesopotamian religion is of primary significance. In order to grasp the nature of the data available for that quest, a short history of the modern archaeological study of the region is important to understand how our knowledge base began, was originally interpreted, and has changed over the last hundred and fifty years.

Short History of the Field

Ancient Mesopotamia was, to a large extent, buried and forgotten over time.[1] Some memories of the Assyrians and Babylonians were preserved

---

1. C. W. Ceram's account, though maybe more adventurous than academic for some, contains an exciting account of the discovery of some of ancient Mesopotamia's key sites and artifacts; *Gods, Graves, and Scholars*, 209-322. For a picture of how the area was forgotten, see esp. 209. For a detailed history of one particular site, including its ancient through its modern reception, with a particular focus on the nineteenth and early twentieth centuries, see Russell, *From Nineveh to New York*.

through the Hebrew Bible[2] and ancient Greek historians.[3] The image preserved in these texts is of a militaristic state ruled by despots controlling bloodthirsty armies with great wealth.[4] It was not the goal of these texts to depict the Sumerians, Assyrians, or Babylonians as "religious" or concerned with larger issues of the universe, and thus few references to any religious practices of Mesopotamia are preserved in this literature. The biblical material, in some cases, even depicts both the Babylonians and the Assyrians as being used by the biblical deity to fulfill that deity's goals.[5]

It was only with the intentional excavation of Mesopotamian sites in the nineteenth century C.E. that our image of ancient Mesopotamia began to change. Suddenly there were monumental reliefs, cuneiform tablets, and ancient buildings casting a new light on who these ancient peoples were and how they lived.[6] These texts provided scholars with new kinds of information. While this was helpful and represented a boon for scholarship, excavation methods were still in their infancy, recording techniques were not yet developed in a scientific way, and the focus and reason for excavating in any particular place often had more to do with political and/or military concerns associated with the excavator than answering scholarly questions. These first excavators viewed this material, as does any scholar, through the social, political, and cultural context of their own civilization. Thus, for example, initial scholarship on Neo-Assyrian religion was generated primarily by British authors who tended to express their vision of this material through the tone of British imperialism.[7] As a result, the initial contact with ancient Mesopotamia, and the groundbreaking fundamental scholarship on the topic, were molded by such a mind-set.

The relationship of the ancient Mesopotamian finds to the Bible as a means for elucidating the biblical text was an initial fascination that governed scholars' understanding of the material. The "Babel/Bible" contro-

2. These appear in the Hebrew Bible, e.g., in 1 and 2 Kings, 1 and 2 Chronicles, Isaiah, and Jeremiah.

3. Berosus, Herodotus. See also Holloway, *Assur Is King! Assur Is King!*, 1.

4. Holloway, *Assur Is King!*, 1.

5. E.g., concerning the exile of northern Israel in 2 Kings 17:7 the text claims, "This happened because the Israelites sinned against the Deity, their God, who had freed them from the land of Egypt." Ironically, the book of Jonah depicts the people of the Assyrian city Nineveh as repentant and accepting of the Israelite prophet's warning.

6. Holloway, *Assur Is King!*, 43-64.

7. Holloway, *Assur Is King!*, 12.

versy that erupted in early-twentieth-century Germany is rooted in the relationship between these two fields.[8] This was true not only for the finds but the interpretation of the cuneiform tablets, especially since two of the earliest translated texts concern a Mesopotamian "parallel" to the flood story,[9] and the Black Obelisk of Shalmaneser III mentions and visually depicts the Israelite king on the top of the monument.[10] How the two fields intersect and should connect is still being discussed in the scholarly arena.[11]

A final issue impacting the initial placement of this material and its early interpretation concerns the relationship of history and archaeology. For much of the early years of the field, the goal of archaeological recovery was based on the needs of the historian, especially those deriving from the *Annales* school of historians. Any discussion of the history of the ancient Near East relates to materials recovered from excavations, but the bulk of this material comes from excavations carried out in the mid-nineteenth to mid-twentieth centuries. Since the middle of the last millennium the emphasis has changed, partially because of financial and political realities but also because of a shift in the scholarly approach employed by many archaeologists. One of the original motivating factors behind site choice for excavation purposes had been to find direct evidence for supplementing and reconstructing history.[12]

Much has changed since the mid-nineteenth century in terms of access to archaeological sites, funding, number of staff, and research design and goals. One shift that impacts our understanding of ancient religion is that ancient Near Eastern archaeologists now are more concerned with the internal archaeological dialogue of interest only to the profession.[13] This is especially reflected in site selection and the periods archaeologists hope to

8. The role of politics and how it impacted who excavated, where, and how they interpreted finds is addressed as background to understanding the "Babel/Bible" debate in Larsen, "The "Babel/Bible" Controversy and Its Aftermath."

9. For example, George Smith's personal account of finding the "flood tablet" conveys some of the excitement and impact of the text; "The Chaldean Account of the Deluge."

10. Holloway, *Assur Is King!*, 19-26.

11. See, e.g., Chavalas and Younger, *Mesopotamia and the Bible*, as just one recent example of different approaches in a volume that grew out of scholarly meetings.

12. Gates, "Archaeology and the Ancient Near East," 65-66.

13. Gates, "Archaeology and the Ancient Near East," 73.

uncover: the focus is more on rural prehistoric and protoliterate sites and/or sites that are not major urban hubs.[14] Furthermore, the questions many archaeologists working in the region seek to address are less concerned with historical problems. This does not mean the data produced is of no use to historians or those trying to understand the role of religion in history, but the quest for data on those specific questions is no longer the driving force.

Finally, political realities impose themselves on where archaeologists can and cannot excavate. In the 1970s, as a result of damming projects along the Tigris and Euphrates rivers, a large number of salvage operations in Syria opened up that country considerably to archaeological investigation. Shortly thereafter, because of the wars in the Persian Gulf, particularly the Persian Gulf War I in 1991, ancient Mesopotamia itself was closed to excavation. Legal excavation of the area has not opened up in any significant way since, and as a result there is not much newly excavated material from dated contexts to add to our understanding of ancient Mesopotamia.

This short overview of the field explains why some of the information that might be helpful concerning specific locations in which the artifacts were found and their relationship to other objects found in the same area, particularly that concerning religious architecture, may not exist. There are questions, even about the data recovered, for which we have no answers, or not satisfactory ones. This does not mean that the information is not used and cannot help, but it explains the status of some of the finds we do have.

Artifacts

There is debate among some scholars as to whether or not all ancient artifacts should be treated the same. As suggested above, the most useful artifacts are those uncovered through legal and scientific excavation. Some scholars, especially those who focus on reading cuneiform tablets, suggest that regardless of whether or not they come from a context excavated by legally conducted archaeological investigation, all tablets are of equal value.[15]

14. Gates, "Archaeology and the Ancient Near East," 66.

15. This is of particular concern because many of the major scholarly scientific journals will not publish the first article about an artifact not discovered through legal

Yet, without context, much about an artifact is lost in terms of its authenticity, when it was used, when it was deposited, the state of its importance when it was last used, and with what other artifacts it was associated.

In recent years the authenticity of many famous artifacts has been questioned, including recent "discoveries" and even artifacts that have been known for close to a century.[16] A number of sensational cases highlight how difficult it is to determine whether or not an artifact is authentic unless it has been discovered through scientific investigation. The "Jesus sarcophagus" may be an example of an ancient artifact that has been inscribed in modern times, creating a hybrid of sorts that is partially ancient but in its present form not completely authentic. Thus only discovery through scientific inquiry ensures the legitimacy of the artifact.

Artifacts discovered through scientific investigation are associated with other objects as well and, hopefully, within secure contexts that allow the investigator to date the context in which it was found through numerous criteria. This becomes relevant even for tablets, because a tablet could carry a date of one particular time period but appear in a much later context. This can indicate a number of things about the tablet — that it was important and so kept, or that it was used for some other reason, often as garbage and filler. This suggests something about when the artifact went out of use and sometimes why.

The associated artifacts often suggest the context in which the artifact was discovered. Thus, finding large numbers of tablets together may reveal some kind of an archive or library. This often depends also on where on the site such materials are discovered. It is not unusual in palaces and cultic contexts to find a room or area with a large number of tablets. In other instances, homes found in apparently residential areas may contain large numbers of different kinds of tablets. This may suggest the occupant of the home is a scribe or a teacher, or there could be some combination of a personal residence with a public function.[17]

Unfortunately, as noted above, in the early days of archaeology in

---

scientific investigation. For example, see the policies for the American Schools of Oriental Research, one of the primary professional organizations for archaeologists working in the modern Middle East: http://www.asor.org/excavations/policy.html.

16. For a catalogue of Mesopotamian artifacts, see Muscarella, *The Lie Became Great.*

17. Zettler, "Written Documents as Excavated Artifacts and the Holistic Interpretation of the Mesopotamian Archaeological Record."

Mesopotamia the guidelines for scientific excavation were not fully developed. While much of the material discovered is considered to be authentic, details that would further help modern scholars understand the ancient context were not recorded. Investigating the notes of the original excavator, if they exist, can help find clues, but this is not always the case. Thus, for many of the texts used in the study of ancient Mesopotamian religion, the original location of the text and other items with which they were discovered is more often than not either not known or not included in the discussion of the text.

The key "problem" with artifacts is that noninscribed archaeological artifacts are silent. They cannot tell modern scholars how they were used, who used them, or what function they served. Archaeologists must rely on the context of the find to determine how some of these artifacts were employed in antiquity. A common joke among many archaeologists is that if they cannot figure out the purpose of the artifact, it must be cultic — in other words, related to something religious. This explains to some extent why much of the information in this book, despite efforts to the contrary, depends on inscriptional material.

Buildings

Buildings are another rich source of data, but they are also silent. A great deal of information can be gleaned from excavating remains of buildings and their groupings into cities. The layout of a building provides information about its use. Yet, like artifacts without an inscription, it is difficult to state categorically what the function of a building was, when it was built, used, and/or went out of use. In fact, over time this could be radically different, especially for buildings that were used for some central function (like temples) and therefore stood for a long period of time. As a result, as with artifacts, while this introduction considers architecture it does not dwell on it.

Tablets

Cuneiform tablets are a wonderful resource, the study of which is fairly recent. Ancient scribes in Mesopotamia wrote on clay tablets, using a reed stylus with a triangular head to create the symbols that made up the ancient words, leading to the modern name "cuneiform" or "wedge-shaped" writing referring to the script. When clay tablets become hard (and in modern times many have been baked for preservation), they become almost indestructible. They can break, however, and words and signs can be broken off, but in general they are well preserved. It often feels to modern scholars that these breaks occur precisely at the "good part" of the text. It is clear that ancient scribes who copied some of these tablets experienced these same problems and either filled in the blanks or indicated that such a loss in the text was already there. Over the last century and a half, thousands of these tablets have been recovered, both from archaeological excavations and through illegal digging.

The early stage in the recovery of these tablets involved an effort to decipher the languages recorded.[18] In more recent years, sign lists,[19] dictionaries,[20] grammars,[21] and introductory volumes have made the process of learning and translating these languages significantly easier.[22] Yet progress in making these languages available to people beyond the field of Assyriology remains limited, especially compared to biblical studies, from which, to some extent, the field originated. As a result, a great amount of scholarly time and energy has been spent simply producing original transcriptions and translations of these documents.

These texts provide a great resource for the history of ancient Mesopotamia and for the religion of the region. In the corpus of texts modern scholars have discovered law codes, myths, love songs, dictionaries, lists of all sorts, omens, and daily receipts. These data provide the basis for our reconstruction of ancient Mesopotamian religion.

Unfortunately, not all of these texts had their original find spots clearly noted in the archaeological report, and therefore for many of them we cannot know where or with what other texts the corpus was found. We

18. Gordon, *Forgotten Scripts.*

19. Labat and Malbran-Labat, *Manuel d'épigraphie akkadienne;* Borger, *Assyrisch-babylonische Zeichenliste.*

20. *Chicago Assyrian Dictionary; Pennsylvania Sumerian Dictionary;* von Soden, *Akkadisches Handwörterbuch; Assyrian-English-Assyrian Dictionary* (the Neo-Assyrian Text Corpus Project); and Black, George, and Postgate, *A Concise Dictionary of Akkadian,* to name some of the more widely used in North America.

21. Von Soden, *Grundriss der akkadischen Grammatik.*

22. Huehnergard, *A Grammar of Akkadian.*

do not know how all of these texts were classified or with what other texts they were grouped in antiquity. Nevertheless, for some there are studies about the location of the finds and what that data can tell us about the texts, and this may provide some insight into how they should be treated.[23]

As a result, while the texts provide most of the data for the outline provided in this volume, there are still questions that cannot be answered based only on texts. We do not usually know who is responsible for the text at hand and even less often its original author, not just the one who inscribed the tablet. Many of the literary pieces are not dated, and most of these ancient texts do not include the name of the author. Such as they are, the texts provide us with a great deal of information, but much that we would like to know remains open to interpretation.

Conclusions

The resources for studying ancient Mesopotamia are many, yet each is fraught with problems and none is complete. In particular, there are no ancient witnesses who sat down to tell us how they felt about most things religious. More often then not, the texts reveal how they acted and how they organized their religious life but seldom why they did things this way. For that reason the focus of this volume is not on how people felt about things, or their deep-seated hopes, dreams, and belief systems, but what they did that would fall under the definition of religion as set forth in the Introduction.

---

23. For an example of what the find spots of a text can add, and a text used in this volume, see Michalowski, *The Lamentation over the Destruction of Sumer and Ur*, 16-19.

CHAPTER 3

History of Mesopotamia

A number of different terms are used when referring to the history of Mesopotamia. Unlike Egypt, which has ancient documentation separating it into dynasties,[1] Mesopotamia has no such self-defined system for referring to its past. In fact, there is not even an Akkadian word that could easily be defined as "history." Thus, the separation of historical periods in Mesopotamia is rooted in classifying periods of political domination which over the past one hundred years modern scholars have gleaned from historical texts. Some of these politically defined historical periods are accompanied by a change in material culture and/or use of language, but other times not.

The goal of this chapter is to provide a skeleton of the flow of history in Mesopotamia in order to contextualize the shifts in religious trends referenced throughout the rest of the volume. Numerous introductions to the history of Mesopotamia can be consulted for a more detailed understanding of the history of Mesopotamia.[2] Here, attention is focused not so much on the reasons for or background of historical shifts, but on the

1. Modern historians accept as a framework the chronological scheme adopted by Manetho, the high priest in Heliopolis who wrote a history of Egypt in the third century B.C.E. While the bulk of his history does not survive, a list of kings and their years of rule preserved in the writings of early Christian chronographers divides Egyptian history into thirty-one dynasties from Menes, the first pharaoh, until the conquest of Alexander the Great in 332; Aldred, *The Egyptians*, 8.

2. To name a few: Roux, *Ancient Iraq*; Kuhrt, *The Ancient Near East c. 3000-330 B.C.*; van de Mieroop, *A History of the Ancient Near East ca. 3000-323*.

components that may have, in this author's opinion, either heavily influenced why a religious change occurred or highlighted such things as influxes of new people to the area or language shifts that influenced religious practice as we understand it.

The first issue is how to break up the periods. Methodologically speaking, I am not following a classic approach to historical periods, documentation, or trends but will cover the areas generally and, at times, separate the history of different areas of Mesopotamia from each other.[3] The pedagogical reason for this approach is that it allows the reader to see the historical development in one area separate from the other, and by seeing the same periods covered twice (in places where there will be overlap) it allows the reader to see vividly how similar historical events influence the cultural and political situation differently. In this context, I will at times review the history separated by place because the trajectory of some of these areas is slightly different.

Ancient Sumer

"Sumer" is the English word derived from the Akkadian term for southern Mesopotamia whose origin is unknown. Technically, "Sumer" is written with the cuneiform signs ki-en-gi, meaning something like "homeland" in Sumerian. Thus, Sumer loosely refers to the southern Tigris-Euphrates Valley, inside the borders of modern Iraq. The native terminology recognized only a Sumerian area and Sumerian language.[4] This means that Sumer is a place and, technically speaking, a Sumerian is a person who lives in Sumer and/or speaks the Sumerian language, to be discussed below.

The prehistory of Mesopotamia is complicated because our data are uneven. While the focus of this unit is history, and history begins with writing, a few components of prehistory will be offered here. The civilization ultimately labeled "Sumerian" (having cultural implications as people

3. Note there are numerous definitions of history and the task of the historian. There is no space in this study for such a thorough discussion, but a good introductory analysis within the ancient Near Eastern context includes Snell, "The Historian's Task," 110-21.

4. Michalowski, "Sumerians," 95.

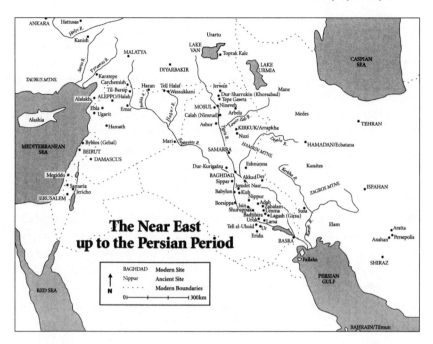

The Near East up to the Persian Period

speaking Sumerian, living in Sumer, and part of a culture that modern scholars label Sumerian) has its roots in the Neolithic developments beginning around 9000 B.C.E., possibly the most important of which was agriculture.[5] One significant result of the development of agriculture is that it allowed societies to build settlements which they could occupy year-round.[6] The growth in technology associated with agriculture led to the development of irrigation systems, allowing the Tigris and Euphrates rivers to be tapped to water fields only when needed. Between 6000 and 5500, irrigation improved to the point where permanent settlement became constant on the lower Mesopotamian plain.[7]

The lack of writing means scholars base their understanding of development in the area purely on archaeological remains, limiting what we can

5. For a general introduction to agriculture in the ancient Near East, see Nissen, *The Early History of the Ancient Near East 9000–2000 B.C.*

6. Van de Mieroop, *A History*, 11.

7. Van de Mieroop, *A History*, 13.

say about the region politically. This is somewhat frustrating for modern scholars, since many significant developments, especially regarding the formation of the people's identity of themselves and their earliest religious practices, develop in this era. These early groups are labeled by the site at which a certain array of similar artifacts was originally discovered. At first it was thought these periods were chronologically sequenced, and later it was determined that some of them overlap. These cultures covered a wide geographical range and date from about 6500-3500 B.C.E. In general order of appearance from oldest to more recent are the cultures/periods of Hassuna/Samarra, Halaf/Early Ubaid, Ubaid, and Uruk.[8]

What is significant for purposes here is that in these periods we first see visible differences between the north and south, the rise of a hierarchy, centralization of powers and functions — all elements that will continue throughout Mesopotamian history.[9] At one time there was discussion about when the Sumerians entered the region, where they originated, and their impact on the region.[10] What has changed significantly about our understanding of these early periods is that there is no cultural break from the beginning of the Ubaid period to the origins of writing. Among the Sumerians there are no traditions of coming from somewhere else.[11] Thus, the Sumerians and the Akkadians (the differences to be discussed below) both appear to be the natural progression of groups in the region for about two thousand years before the appearance of written texts.

The Late Uruk period marks a significant point because it was then that the first written records appear. Other important developments include state and city formation, specialized labor, mass production, cylinder seals, and, of central concern here, ceremonial sanctuaries. These complexes are set on large platforms, with elaborate approaches, some built of stone. The walls are decorated with mosaic patterns made up of small cones with yellow, black, or red painted on the visible ends, and are associated with a range of objects such as stone vases and inlaid or worked relief statuary.[12] Again, important for understanding religion in Mesopotamia is

---

8. Van de Mieroop, *A History,* 15.

9. Van de Mieroop, *A History,* 15.

10. A discussion of the "Sumerian Problem" that summarizes the problems involved is found in Roux, *Ancient Iraq,* 85-89. Newer histories of the region such as van de Mieroop and Kuhrt no longer refer to the "problem."

11. Black and Green, *Gods, Demons and Symbols of Ancient Mesopotamia,* 11.

12. Kuhrt, *The Ancient Near East,* 27.

that sanctuaries and their leaders appear early on in Mesopotamia's development, and thus they shape the core of the religious system.

The Uruk period leads into the Early Dynastic period, which is usually divided into three eras: ED I (ca. 2900-2800), ED II (2800-2600), and ED III (2600-2334 B.C.E.), though, like the prehistoric period, the divisions between some of these appear now to be more geographical than temporal.[13] With this period Mesopotamian events can now be deemed somewhat "historical" insofar as there are now written narratives from some of the rulers and many administrative texts. While the royal inscriptions in many cases consist only of the name of the ruler and corresponding city, later Mesopotamian literature refers to some of these figures; thus having historical documentation of this person becomes especially important in understanding the development of Mesopotamian literature and its relationship to history and historical figures.

The city-state was the basic political unit in the Early Dynastic period.[14] In the early third millennium, southern Mesopotamia saw a general population growth, leading to growth in the cities. With regard to religion, the concept of the city is significant in this period because the cities were considered to have developed for the gods. Each city had a patron deity, the temple was the home of the deity (and that deity's wealth), and the priest was in charge of the deity's house and therefore the city.[15]

The growth of the cities led to their boundaries encroaching upon neighboring cities, which led, more often than not, to hostilities. Thus, a leader's military prowess became more important. As a result, this period reflects a growth in a new military class and a new building type: the palace.[16] Despite the growth of more power in a military leader, the city still belonged to a deity, and therefore battles between cities were also battles between deities.[17]

Towards the end of the ED III period, the cities of Mesopotamia were fighting with each other, forming alliances, and yet despite this, they have some sense of unity. Though each city had its own patron deity, that deity

---

13. Dates are from van de Mieroop, *A History,* 39-40.

14. Michalowski, "Sumerians," 97.

15. Van de Mieroop, *A History,* 43.

16. Van de Mieroop, *A History,* 45.

17. For a helpful introduction to the inscriptions and translation of some of the key texts, see Magid, "Sumerian Early Dynastic Royal Inscriptions."

did not exist in a void but was part of a larger pantheon of deities. Some deities had more power than others, yet this was not necessarily based on whether or not that particular city was the strongest. The city of Nippur is a particular case in point. Nippur was the seat of Enlil, the chief Mesopotamian deity in the third and early second millennium, though there is no evidence that Nippur was ever important militarily. In the Early Dynastic period, kings of Adab, Kish, Lagash, Umma, and Uruk left inscriptions there, apparently seeking legitimacy through Nippur.[18]

The Early Dynastic period ends with the arrival of Sargon (2334-2279 B.C.E.), who created the first politically unified Mesopotamian state, one that was maintained with dynastic control through four successive rulers.[19] Sargon's allure went beyond just being the first ruler to unify Mesopotamia, as can be seen from the numerous legends surrounding him in later times.[20] In his own time, Sargon shifted the nature of politics in the region from intercity warfare, centralizing Mesopotamia in a number of ways that led the region to control and influence a much larger geographical region. Texts suggest that much of his power came from his military, noting that "daily 5,400 men ate at his presence."[21] Sargon and his heirs campaigned from Syria to Iran, and their commercial ties linked them to Anatolia, the Mediterranean, and the Indus Valley.[22] Sargon moved his capital to Akkad, a site which has not yet been identified by modern scholars.

The larger area of rule demanded that Sargon create a new government. The original city-rulers appear to have remained in place but now functioned as governors. A new system of taxation was implemented to support the centralized government, and later a standard system of weights and measures was introduced.[23] Ideological and theological modifications occurred as well, especially in the realm of religion when Sargon appointed his daughter, Enheduanna, as high priestess of the moon-god Nanna at Ur.[24]

Possibly the most striking shift implemented by Sargon and carried out by his successors was the introduction of Akkadian, a Semitic language

18. Van de Mieroop, *A History,* 49.
19. Van de Mieroop, *A History,* 64.
20. Westenholz, *Legends of the Kings of Akkade,* 1.
21. Frayne, *Sargonic and Gutian Period (2334-2113 BC),* 31.
22. Westenholz, *Legends of the Kings of Akkade,* 1.
23. Weiss, "Akkade," 42.
24. Kuhrt, *The Ancient Near East,* 50.

which had apparently been more prominent in the northern area of the Babylonian plain where Sargon originated, as the official language of the state. The name comes from that of Sargon's capital, Akkad (Agade).[25] Previously the majority of royal and state inscriptions had been in Sumerian,[26] the earliest written language yet discovered, written in cuneiform,[27] and presumably spoken, in Mesopotamia in the third millennium B.C.E.[28]

By the end of the third millennium the "land of Akkad" referred, in general, to northern Babylonia, from north of Nippur to Sippar. Just as many other ancient terms broadened in use, during the second millennium it came to designate the indigenous population of all of Babylonia, as opposed to the nomadic Amorites.[29] People with Akkadian names already appear in the first tablets written in Sumerian.[30]

As a Semitic language Akkadian is closely related to contemporary languages in the area.[31] At issue, especially in trying to understand the distinction between deities with both Akkadian and Sumerian names, is what, if anything beyond language, distinguished a Sumerian from an Akkadian. Because the early history of cuneiform is still poorly documented, all we can state categorically is that Sumer was not a linguistically homogenous area but that Sumerian dominated in official discourse prior to the rule of Sargon and his descendants.[32]

Sargon's sons and successors, Rimush and Manishtushu, and his grandson Naram-Sin devoted much of their time suppressing revolts in Sumerian cities and expanding the borders of the state. Both of Sargon's sons were murdered. Like Sargon, a great deal of legendary literature grew up around Naram-Sin. In contrast to Sargon, the later texts depict Naram-Sin in a particularly negative light, suggesting that the Dynasty of Akkad ended with him — at least in part, according to the "Curse of Agade" — because he removed goods and divine statues from Nippur, Enlil's city.[33]

---

25 Huehnergard, "Akkadian," 44.

26. Michalowski, "Sumerians," 97.

27. Sumerian is not related to any other known language, ancient or modern; Civil, "Sumerian," 92.

28. Michalowski, "Sumerians," 97.

29 Foster, "Akkadians," 49.

30. Black and Green, *Gods, Demons and Symbols,* 11.

31, Huehnergard, "Akkadian," 44.

32. Michalowski, "Sumerians," 97.

33. Cooper, *The Curse of Agade,* 142-63. For more on the important religious signif-

The historical outline of Naram-Sin's reign shows that there was much campaigning during his reign. He continued Sargon's policy of appointing a royal daughter to the cultic role in Ur, and royal relatives were installed as governors.[34]

Evidence suggests that the negative evaluation of Naram-Sin in the literary tradition is erroneous, in particular because his son ruled for twenty-five years, and also there is evidence of temple-building in his reign.[35] The question then turns to why he may have drawn the ire of later writers. One possibility is that this negative tradition originates in the following Ur III period as part of the ideological justification for the succeeding reign.[36] Another reason, not necessarily disconnected, may be rooted in the deification of Naram-Sin during his lifetime. One inscription reads, "(Naram-Sin) be made a god, and then built his temple in the midst of (the city of) Agade."[37] (This will be considered in more detail in Chapter 10, "Kingship, Religion, and the Gods.")

Naram-Sin was succeeded by his son Sharkalisharri, though little is known about his twenty-five-year reign. Sumerian tradition lays the reasons for the final collapse of Sargonic rule upon a group named the Gutians,[38] though internal weakness and rebellion are also possibilities.[39]

The Sumerian King List includes about one hundred names of Gutian rulers who ruled the following period, best summed up in the list's comment, "Who was king? Who was not king?"[40] Despite reference to attack and rule by outsiders, the southern Mesopotamian city-states appear to have reverted to local rule. In inscriptions, Utuhegal, ruler of the city of Uruk, recounts his battles with the Gutians and claims to return kingship to Sumer.

Ur-Namma (previously called Ur-Nammu), was Utuhegal's military governor at Ur and took over the kingship, eventually reuniting all of Sumer in what scholars call the Neo-Sumerian Renaissance, the Neo-

---

icance of the cult of Enlil at Nippur, see Chapter 5 on the pantheon and the discussion of Enlil.

34. Kuhrt, *The Ancient Near East,* 50.
35. Kuhrt, *The Ancient Near East,* 50.
36. Kuhrt, *The Ancient Near East,* 58.
37. Michalowski, "Mortal Kings of Ur," 34.
38. Michalowski, "Sumerians," 98.
39. Foster, "Akkadians," 53.
40. Sumerian King List, col. vii, line 1. See Jacobsen, *The Sumerian King List,* 113.

Sumerian period, or Ur III (ca. 2112-2004 B.C.E.). Apart from these modern designations, while the bureaucratic and literary language of the dynasty was Sumerian, much of how the state was governed grew directly out of the centralized practices initiated in the Sargonic period. In fact, under Ur-Namma's son and successor Shulgi, Mesopotamia became centralized even more. Shulgi reinstituted the official language and writing system, reorganized weights and measures, taxation, the military, and the religious sector. Shulgi, as had Naram-Sin, deified himself (see Chapter 10 below). Shulgi also had many wives and arranged marriages for his children to solidify political alliances and offices.[41]

Despite all efforts at consolidation to enforce stability and control, the Ur III period continued to be a time of warfare, and the kingdom fell after a brief century of rule. As was the case with the Sargonic period, it is possible that reasons for the collapse included an overextended bureaucracy, expensive military, and weakening of central control, though outside forces, especially the appearance of a people known as the Amorites, and a final invasion of a group from Iran contributed to the end.[42] The close of the Ur III period marked the end of Sumerian as a bureaucratic language. It is unclear whether Sumerian was actually spoken in this period, but after this time it survived largely as a scholarly enterprise. The demise of the Sumerian language is not solely a linguistic turning point, but it was a historical moment signifying, on some levels, the end of an era as it stands at the dawn of another. The magnitude of this event was recognized by the ancient author of a text known by its modern title, *Lamentation over the Destruction of Sumer and Ur.*[43]

Assyria and Babylon

With the disappearance of Sumerian as a spoken and/or political language, the terminology used to refer to the regions in Mesopotamia shifts. In the second millennium, partially because of the influx of the new people known as the Amorites combined with the demise of Sumerian, scholarship no longer refers to Sumer and Akkad but rather Assyria and

41. Michalowski, "Sumerians," 99.
42. Michalowski, "Sumerians," 99.
43. Michalowski, *The Lamentation over the Destruction of Sumer and Ur.*

Babylonia. The terms "Assyrian" and "Babylonian" refer to inhabitants of Mesopotamia from the second through the middle of the first millennium B.C.E. The Babylonians occupy the southern part of the flood plain and the Assyrians the north, though these geographical designations do not reflect the complex differences between the two concerning language, their historical connection to the Sumerians, political configurations, and religion.

Babylonia

The Babylonians occupied the region extending approximately from modern Baghdad to the shore of the Persian Gulf. The name is derived from the city named "Babili" in cuneiform, which becomes Babylon in Greek.[44] This area coincides mostly with the area occupied by the Sumerians in the third millennium. As noted above, the Third Dynasty of Ur fell due to a series of events concerning economic and political instability and the influx of a new group of people to the area: the Amorites.

The first two centuries of the second millennium, the Isin/Larsa period, saw a number of transitional groups try to gain control of Mesopotamia, with limited success.[45] The cultural and religious traditions of the previous millennium were preserved and modified[46] despite the entrance of this people grouped under the name Amorites.[47] Only under Hammurabi did Babylon gain control of all Mesopotamia.[48]

The period in which Hammurabi dominated Mesopotamia is referred to as the Old Babylonian period. Babylon under Hammurabi slowly picked off the other city-states until he controlled the entire region. The site of Babylon at this time presently lies beneath the water table, so much of our knowledge of this period is from other sites, particularly that of Mari. At this site, Tell Hariri, archaeologists since 1933 have excavated a large town with its palaces still retaining their painted walls as well as some

---

44. Klengel-Brandt, "Babylonians," 256.

45. Van Koppen, "Old Babylonian Period Inscriptions."

46. Sjoberg, "The Old Babylonian Eduba"; Buccellati, "Through a Tablet Darkly."

47. Heimpel, *Letters to the King of Mari;* Schwartz, "Pastoral Nomadism in Ancient Western Asia."

48. Horsnell, *The Year-Names of the First Dynasty of Babylon.*

fifteen thousand tablets.[49] Many of these are letters that date from the period of Amorite domination and Mari's last ruler, Zimri-Lim, a contemporary of Hammurabi's. This archive is important for many reasons, particularly because the numerous texts offer insight into daily life, administrative relationships between the king and his servants in the cities under Mari's control, and relationships among the various kingdoms contemporary with Hammurabi.[50]

Hammurabi is the best-known name from this period because of his military and political successes, which forever changed the role and status of Babylon and its god Marduk, to some extent serving to identify and create the group labeled Babylonians. Hammurabi's heirs did not rule with the same authority as Hammurabi, and in 1595 Babylon was sacked in a raid by the Hittites. The Hittites did not stay to control Babylon, but they did take with them the statue of the city god Marduk.[51]

Even before the Hittites arrived, in the reign of Hammurabi's son and successor, Samsu-ilum, two new groups had entered the region of Babylonia. In the south a new dynasty, the Sealand Dynasty, came to power under Iluma-ilum, and in his ninth year he mentions another new group, the Kassites.[52] The origin of the Kassites is unclear, as is the reason for their appearance in Babylonia, but they controlled Babylon politically for the next four hundred years.[53] Little is known about their language as they adopted Babylonian language and customs fairly quickly. While the Kassites are always treated as somehow non-Babylonian, and most scholars argue that little influence of their national characteristics is reflected in the material remains of their occupation,[54] the Kassites reigned some four centuries, "far longer than any native or for that matter any other dynasty."[55] Babylonian literature flourished during this time, with some important Mesopotamian texts appearing to date to this period.[56] The Kassites may have negotiated the return of Marduk, and there is evidence

49. Margueron, "Mari," 413.

50. Margueron, "Mari," 415.

51. Foster, "Agum-Kakirme and the Return of Marduk," *Before the Muses,* 1:273-77.

52. Horsnell, *The Year-Names,* 192.

53. Brinkman, *A Catalogue of Cuneiform Sources Pertaining to Specific Monarchs of the Kassite Dynasty.*

54. Lloyd, *The Archaeology of Mesopotamia,* 172.

55. Oates, *Babylon,* 86.

56. Foster, "The Mature Period," *Before the Muses,* 1:203-9.

that the text *Enuma Elish*, which makes an important contribution to understanding the Mesopotamian concept of the world, was written in connection with this event.[57]

The Euphrates took a dramatic westward shift towards the end of the Kassite period, or shortly thereafter, as a result of the sustained and gradual effects of salinization combined with a sudden change in hydrological resources.[58] This led to the reduction of population in Babylonian cities. Taking advantage of these environmental concerns, the Assyrians began to threaten Babylonia. Significant in this regard is the conquest of Babylonia by Tukulti-Ninurta I in 1235.[59] This conquest of Babylon was not prolonged, but its effects were. It marks the beginning of both the Assyro-Babylonian conflict and the significant Babylonian cultural influence on Assyria. The Kassites were destroyed shortly thereafter in an Elamite raid in which Babylon was again sacked and many of her artifacts taken to Susa, where they were discovered by French archaeologists in the nineteenth century.[60]

In the three hundred years following the fall of the Kassites, Babylonia was controlled by a series of dynasties featuring rulers of various ethnic components, none of which were new to the area. Nebuchadnezzar I (1124-1103 B.C.E.) began a new phase of Babylonian history when he attacked the Elamites and recovered the statue of Marduk taken earlier in the sack of Babylon. He referred to Marduk as "king of the gods," possibly elevating the deity to a new status as chief of the Babylonian pantheon.[61] The Arameans entered the area around this time, disrupting internal stability, as reflected in the paucity of excavated documents. The rise of the Assyrians towards the end of the tenth century was accompanied by the appearance of the Chaldeans[62] in the south, which led a Babylonian chron-

---

57. See the discussion of that text below.

58. Brinkman, *Prelude to Empire*, 3-10; Adams, *The Heartland of Cities*, 18, 152, 155-58.

59. Grayson, *Assyrian Rulers of the Third and Second Millennia* BC. For the Tukulti-Ninurta Epic, see Foster, *Before the Muses*, 1:209-29.

60. Dieulafoy, "A History of Excavation at Susa"; also Arevalier, "The French Scientific Delegation in Persia."

61. "The Seed of Kingship," line 25, in Foster, *Before the Muses*, 1:292.

62. Delineating the differences between the Chaldeans and the Arameans is not easy, though the ancient sources do so. See Arnold, "What Has Nebuchadnezzar to Do With David."

icle to claim, "there was no king in the land."[63] Yet despite the impact of the Arameans on the area and the political instability around 1200, much Babylonian literature was now standardized.[64]

Conflict between Assyria and Babylonia continued throughout the period of Assyrian hegemony of the ancient Near East, from the end of the tenth century through the demise of Assyria in the late seventh century. When Assyria was weaker, as in the period following the reign of Adad-Nirari III, the Chaldeans filled the political vacuum. When Assyria was stronger, their kings employed a variety of strategies to impose power over the region. For example, Sennacherib destroyed Babylon and took Marduk with him to Assyria.[65] Esarhaddon, following his father Sennacherib's assassination, tried to deal with the Babylonians through appeasement.[66] Yet regardless of the tactic, the Assyrians achieved little success in their efforts to control Babylonia.

Though local Babylonian rulers of various backgrounds maintained limited control, often with the help of Assyria, ancient historians hail Nabonassar as beginning a new era of Babylonian power (748-747 B.C.E.). Beginning with his reign, ancient scholars sought to keep precise records of historical events, as exemplified in the Neo-Babylonian chronicle series.[67]

Following the death of Assurbanipal, the last significant Assyrian ruler, Nabopolassar (626-605) took the throne and established a new Babylonian dynasty that, to some extent, inherited the Assyrian Empire. His son, Nebuchadnezzar, adopted the Assyrian goal of controlling Egypt. It is in response to his campaigns that Judah revolted, leading Nebuchadnezzar to destroy Jerusalem and exile her people (2 Kings 24-25). Nebuchadnezzar was also responsible for major building projects in Babylon and making it a major economic and administrative center.[68]

Nebuchadnezzar's reign was followed by three kings who had no major military or building successes. Nabonidus, with no hereditary claim to

63. Grayson, *Assyrian and Babylonian Chronicles*, Chronicle 24; Glassner, *Mesopotamian Chronicles*.

64. Foster, *Before the Muses*, 1:207.

65. Luckenbill, *The Annals of Sennacherib*, 78.

66. For an analysis of the different means of his policy, see Porter, *Images, Power, Politics*.

67. Grayson, *Assyrian and Babylonian Chronicles*, 10-24 and 69-111.

68. Herodotus, *History* 1.186; Berossus 27 in Josephus, *Ant.* 10.11.1.226; Koldewey, *Excavations at Babylon*; George, "Babylon Revisited," 734-39.

the throne, came to power already aged. He is known for his devotion to Sin, the moon-god of Haran, likely influenced by his mother, Adad-guppi, whose tomb inscription has been preserved.[69] What impact this had on his decision to depart Babylon for ten years while he stayed in the Arabian oasis town of Teima, leaving Babylon unable to carry out the New Year festival, is debated.[70] Shortly after Nabonidus's return, the city fell to Cyrus of Persia, marking the end of Babylonian rule and so this account of Babylonian religion.[71]

Assyria

Assyrian history follows a different trajectory, though it intersects with Babylonian history and culture at a number of points. The early history of the city of Assur is unknown because of a lack of inscriptional evidence, though all texts indicate the area of Assyria was controlled by the Sumerian and Akkadian south.[72]

A summary of early kings, according to the Assyrian King List, the earliest extant exemplar of which dates to the first millennium B.C.E.,[73] lists seventeen kings who lived in tents, ten ancestor kings, six early kings, and six early Old Assyrian kings, with genealogies.[74] Research on this list reveals that, like the Sumerian King list,[75] it serves propagandistic purposes, probably to legitimate the reign of Shamshi-Adad, and shares common Amorite attributes with ancestors of the Hammurabi dynasty. As a result, the data provide more information about how the Assyrians later situated themselves than about actual historical leaders.[76] Despite its problems, a number of rulers from this list appear on inscriptions from Assur and are mentioned in the texts from the Assyrian trading colony at Karum Kanesh,

69. Longman, "The Adad-guppi Autobiography," 477-78.

70. Beaulieu, *The Reign of Nabonidus, King of Babylon, 556-539 B.C.*, 178-85.

71. Herodotus, 1.178, 190-291; Xenophon, *Cyropaedia* 7.5.26-30; Dan. 5:30-31; Glassner, *Mesopotamian Chronicles*, 237; Cogan, "Cyrus Cylinder."

72. For an example, see Steinkeller, "Administrative and Economic Organization of the Ur III State."

73. Poebel, "The Assyrian King List from Khorsabad."

74. Larsen, *The Old Assyrian City-State and Its Colonies*, 36.

75. Jacobsen, *The Sumerian King List*.

76. Larsen, *The Old Assyrian City-State*, 36.

or Kultepe in modern-day Turkey.[77] The documents from Kultepe provide more information about this period in Assyria than any remains from Assur itself.[78] Both sets of documents reveal a city ruled by a person identified as the *isiak assur* or *ensi Assur,* not the Akkadian term for "king," in concert with city elders.[79]

Assyria became a major factor in Mesopotamia under Shamshi-Adad.[80] Shamshi-Adad was not a native-born Assyrian, and while Assyrian rulers neither prior to nor following him took the title king, they came to accept him as one of their own.[81] Shamshi-Adad dominated Mesopotamia from 1813 to 1781.

Assyria was not affected by rival groups to the extent Babylonia had been during the second millennium, but nevertheless competed with and was influenced by the Hurrians.[82] Only with Assur-uballit (1363-1328) did Assyria's leaders claim the title of "king."[83] Assur-uballit began by ousting the Hurrians[84] and placed Assyria on the international stage, a period dominated by the Hittites, Egyptians, and Babylonians. He was followed by a number of strong kings under whose leadership Assyria maintained its role as an important power in the ancient Near East.

Many of the ancient Near Eastern powers of the mid-second millennium fell apart towards the end of the twelfth century, and new peoples, such as the Arameans, entered the area, modifying what constituted an Assyrian.[85]

77. Larsen, *The Old Assyrian City-State,* 37-43. For inscriptions of the pre-Shamshi-Adad kings, see Grayson, *Assyrian Rulers of the Third and Second Millennia BC,* 7-46.

78. Despite difficulties in the publication of these materials, a new series, Old Assyrian Archives, is making more of these data available. See, e.g., Larsen, *The Aššur-nādā Archive.*

79. Larsen, *The Old Assyrian City-State,* 109-59.

80. Villard, "Shamshi-Adad and Sons." For his inscriptions, see Grayson, *Assyrian Rulers of the Third and Second Millennia BC,* 47-76.

81. E.g., the next king to take the title "king," Assur-uballit, refers back to Shamshi-Adad as a king of Assyria; Grayson, *Assyrian Rulers of the Third and Second Millennia BC,* 115-16.

82. Wilhelm, *The Hurrians.*

83. Grayson, *Assyrian Rulers of the Third and Second Millennia BC,* inscription A.0.73.6, 115. Note reference to him as king of Assyria in letters to the Amarna king of Egypt, Akhenaten; Moran, *The Amarna Letters,* EA 15, line 3, and 16.3.

84. Harrak, *Assyria and Hanigalbat.*

85. Ward and Joukowsky, *The Crisis Years.* For the Arameans, see in the same vol-

Assyria began its recovery with Adad-Nirari II (911-891), whose grandson, Assurnasirpal II, took Assyria onto the stage as a world power. Assurnasirpal II expanded the borders of Assyria considerably and began to change the concept of what Assyria was.[86] This expansion brought Assyria into more sustained contact with peoples and cultures outside the traditional boundaries of Assyria. Assurnasirpal II also moved the capital from the traditional home of their national deity Assur in the city of Assur to Calah (modern Nimrud). Shalmaneser III (858-824) further stretched the boundaries of Assyria, but his reign ended in turmoil with some of the major cities, including Assur, revolting.[87] One of his sons, Shamshi-Adad V, managed to regain control of Assyria, but the extent and power of the state diminished so much that the king's underlings wrote their own inscriptions,[88] without even mentioning the king they served.[89]

When Tiglath-Pileser III took the throne he expanded the borders of Assyria through his campaigns and also instituted a number of internal changes.[90] He transformed the army from a solely Assyrian force into a standing army by incorporating conquered peoples, thereby modifying the definition of what and who constituted an Assyrian. Many Assyrian kings prior to his reign practiced deporting conquered communities, but Tiglath-Pileser III established this as a standard policy. The biblical text and Tiglath-Pileser III's inscriptions both refer to the annexation of parts of northern Israel, further modifying the population of Assyria.[91]

Assyria controlled most of the ancient Near East under the reigns of these kings: Shalmaneser V, Sargon II, Sennacherib, Esarhaddon, and Ashurbanipal. Each king was responsible for significant military and political feats, though the cumulative effect was that Assyria was at war for most of this period, her capital shifted periodically, and the nature of the relationship with the conquered peoples evolved. One of Assyria's biggest problems was controlling Babylonia. Various methods were used, from to-

---

ume, Sader, "The 12th Century B.C. in Syria," and the response by McClellan, "12th Century B.C. Syria." See also Lipiński, *The Aramaeans*.

86. Grayson, *Assyrian Rulers of the Early First Millennium BC*.

87. Grayson, *Assyrian Rulers of the Early First Millennium BC*, 2:180-88.

88. See discussion in Grayson, *Assyrian Rulers of the Early First Millennium*, 1:200-1.

89. Thureau-Dangin, "L'inscription des lions de Til-Barsib."

90. Tadmor, *The Inscriptions of Tiglath-Pileser III, King of Assyria*.

91. Summary Inscription 4, obv. lines 15-17 (Tadmor, *The Inscriptions of Tiglath-Pileser III*); 2 Kgs 15:29.

tal destruction of the city[92] to rebuilding the city and employing Babylonian iconography.[93] Assyria's last major ruler, Assurbanipal, built a significant library and museum in which he gathered as much literature as he could amass.[94] Archaeologists uncovered this library early in the discovery of Assyria, and as a result scholars have access to a great deal of Mesopotamian literature. Assur-uballit II was Assyria's last ruler, and with him the Assyrians disappear as a group from the political stage.

Conclusions

This extremely brief discussion of Mesopotamian history is meant to provide students with a general idea of who these different groups were, when they entered the area, what impact they had on its culture, and the names of some of the more important rulers. It is not meant as a thorough survey of Mesopotamian history.

What the review does show is a core set of people in the area who regularly were overrun by or introduced to new groups entering the area. These new groups usually brought with them new languages but not new writing systems. Their impact is not always easy to discern, since usually by the time we encounter them they are already writing in Akkadian, or at least using the cuneiform system of writing, and so have already been incorporated into the Mesopotamian states and administrations.

92. Luckenbill, *The Annals of Sennacherib*, 78.

93. For an analysis of the different means of his policy, see Porter, *Images, Power, Politics*.

94. Oppenheim, *Ancient Mesopotamia*, 15-18.

CHAPTER 4

Myths

Mythology[1]

Ancient Mesopotamians normally did not describe *why* they acted as they did; instead, they recorded *what* they did. Thus, their mythology is one of the few sources that might provide some insight into their religious beliefs. In these texts, some fundamental questions approached by other religious systems are entertained: for example, why are humans here, why do some people die young, and what awaits us after death?

Mythology is a complicated topic because the term is difficult to define and the history of its usage biases the average Western reader even before having a chance to study the myths under discussion. Mythology is presented in a separate chapter here because, to a large extent, much of what modern scholars suggest is at the heart of Mesopotamian religious thought comes from an analysis of this literary genre. At the same time, using these texts is fraught with complications in terms of when and why they were created in the first place, who was supposed to read them, and how well they reflect how Mesopotamians viewed their world. In order to determine how to define this group of texts and how to use them appropriately, this chapter begins with a short discussion of mythology, the his-

---

1. The definition of myth is complex. Here mythology will be vaguely defined as a narrative that describes human understanding of the divine realm as explanation for how and why the universe functions as it does, including the divine relationship to humans and their place in the cosmos.

tory of the term in scholarship, and the particular problems posed by the ancient Near Eastern material.

The approach towards mythology in this chapter does not pretend to cover all the myths available or to categorize them. Instead, the attempt is to show how the mythological texts cover some of the issues that are often raised when discussing religion, such as theology, life and death, and the origins of the world. Since, as shown in the previous chapter, the history of Mesopotamia changed significantly over the two thousand years under discussion, so did the myths and the deities prominent in them. Accordingly, the myths will be examined not as one final document or statement about the universe, which the Mesopotamians never created, but as an ever-changing series of texts that were modified in different periods and places for a range of reasons.

One problem with examining different types of data separately rather than general religious themes is that there will be overlap. Most of the major deities are relevant for all the data sets. On some levels, it might make sense to provide a chapter on the deities first so that the reader has some general understanding of the various deities before seeing how they appear in the texts. However, much of what we know about them, or their actions, comes from the myths and other types of texts that mention them. For this reason, this author will approach myths first to alert the reader to the problems we encounter in trying to understand the gods before introducing the deities and their characteristics.

What Is Myth?

From an anthropological perspective, "myth" is usually treated in terms of its function in ordering or explaining the world for the society in which it was produced.[2] The history of the word and its use in the academy, especially concerning the ancient Near Eastern material, complicate that simple approach.

"Myth" is the English derivative of a Greek word, *mythos*. The Greek term, as used in the late fifth century B.C.E., carried the sense of invented

2. Holm, "Ancient Near Eastern Literature," 273, quoting G. S. Kirk, *Myth: Its Meaning and Functions in Ancient and Other Cultures* (Berkeley: University of California Press, 1970).

Tablet 11 of the Assyrian version of the Gilgamesh Epic (ca. 650 B.C.E.), found at Nineveh.
(Courtesy, The British Museum)

or fictional stories and represented the opposite of the truth, which could be verified or falsified by logic.[3] In 1764, German Hellenist Gottlieb Christian Heyne adopted the term and adapted it for modern scholarly use, making Greek mythology the paradigm and norm for discussing myth. Heyne's usage grew out of confrontation between Greek myths and the

3. Graf, "Myth," 45.

traditional stories of newly-discovered ethnological cultures, which initially did not take the Greek myths seriously. In response, Heyne elevated the status of these narratives, viewing them as primeval human thinking about the world and the repository of human memories.[4] When the ancient Near Eastern corpus was discovered and translated, the texts were not treated as part of the larger body of myths, to be studied as a category, but as a corollary to the Old Testament.[5]

The treatment of myth as ancient theology prevails for some treatments of the ancient Near Eastern material. Thorkild Jacobsen claimed the Mesopotamian myths and epics were existential critiques in which man took stock of himself and the universe around him.[6] Jean Bottéro suggests that in societies that can only think in images and not in abstract terms all those operations (presumably operations forced to think in the abstract) derive from a type of "calculated imagination" we call mythology. He defines myth as "an intellectual procedure which consists of responding to the great questions about the origins and the meaning of the universe and our existence, as well as the role and the activity of the gods, who are considered to have directed everything."[7] He further claims this procedure is not worked out by rational and conceptual analysis to find the truth but to give answers that, while improbable, are sufficient.[8]

Clearly A. Leo Oppenheim was reacting against such thought about mythology in his discussion as to why a Mesopotamian Religion should not be written. He argues:

> To state at the outset my objection to the direct and indiscriminate utilization of such texts, I submit that their contents have already unduly encroached upon our concept of Mesopotamian religion. All these stories about the gods and their doings, about this world of ours and how it came into being, these moralizing as well as entertaining stories geared to emotional responses represent the most obvious and cherished topics for the literary creativeness of a civilization such as that of Mesopotamia. They form something like a fantastic screen, enticing as they are in

---

4. Graf, "Myth," 46.
5. Graf, "Myth," 47.
6. Jacobsen, *The Treasures of Darkness*, 223.
7. Bottéro, *Mesopotamia*, 269.
8. Bottéro, *Mesopotamia*, 298.

their immediate appearance, seductive in their far-reaching lines to stories told all over the ancient Near East and around the Mediterranean,
but still a screen which one must penetrate to reach the hard core of evidence that bears directly on the forms of religious experience of
Mesopotamian man.[9]

He continues by noting that Classical scholars have learned to bypass
the "screen created by mythology" and "utilize what information it may
convey," but strongly suggests those in the field of Mesopotamian studies
have fallen victim to its lure. Finally, he argues these literary formulations
are the work of Sumerian court poets and Old Babylonian scribes imitat-
ing the texts because they are interested in exploiting the artistic possibilities of a new literary language and highlights why these texts should be
studied as literature rather than by historians of religion.[10]

With such a range of strong scholarly emotion on both sides, navigat-
ing the category is clearly fraught with problems. Despite the difficulties
with this genre of literature, it is one category of texts that addresses some
of the key issues many would consider "religious" in nature. Therefore, the
category cannot be completely jettisoned but must be approached with
great caution. The mythological texts will be treated here as literary documents addressing both fundamental issues pertaining to the nature of the
universe and the role of humans within it, while at the same time understanding they are literary documents, produced by scribes with literary aspirations as well as individuals situated in a time and a place where politics
or pride in one's own city may take precedence over tradition or earlier belief systems.

Mesopotamian Myths

Many of the myths from Mesopotamia that have been discovered are copies of earlier texts and date as early as the second millennium, and the
myths may continue in some form for more than a thousand years. The
characters and their actions within these similar documents may change
over time, depicting different, sometimes even contrasting, images or rep-

9. Oppenheim, *Ancient Mesopotamia*, 177.
10. Oppenheim, *Ancient Mesopotamia*, 177.

resentations of a concept. There may also be contemporary myths that seem to depict the same deity in very different terms. It is therefore significant to note that ancient Mesopotamian religion was not dogmatic or systematic.[11]

The lack of a systematic dogma is rooted, to some extent, in the difference between polytheism and monotheism. "Monotheism" and "polytheism" are recent terms, used no earlier than the seventeenth century, and their difference is not purely quantitative. Monotheism in general refers to religions that worship only one deity. This practice is usually accompanied by a text providing instructions for how to live according to the desires of that one deity. Monotheism further asserts its identity by opposing itself to polytheism. One definition of polytheism is the worship of many deities, but this does not mean that there is not some concept of a unity, structure, and coherence to the divine world which impacts the human world.[12] This means that for the present discussion of "mythology" in a polytheistic religion a deity cannot be spoken about without reference to other deities.[13]

For those in the West raised in a predominantly monotheistic society where the religion's history is recorded in an authoritative book — that, at some point, became somewhat codified, though still open to interpretation — the fluctuations in the myths are difficult to understand. How can a deity act one way and be related to one set of deities in one text and appear radically different, even with contradictory parentage, in another? The problem is rooted in Oppenheim's claim that we do not know what the role of these texts was for the ancients. The difficulty lies in trying to force the mythological material into a model that reflects something that appears coherent to us. No known texts from ancient Mesopotamia reflect on the confusion stemming from so many conflicting myths. Some texts do note the uncertainty of determining the deities' wishes,[14] which may be observed also in the Hebrew Bible.[15]

Mythological texts from Mesopotamia cover a wide range of topics. The brief overview at hand is not intended to show how they define

---

11. Collins, "Cosmology," 59.

12. Assman, "Monotheism and Polytheism," 17.

13. Assman, "Monotheism and Polytheism," 19.

14. E.g., the so called "Babylonian Theodicy", Lambert, *Babylonian Wisdom Literature*, 71-91.

15. Cf. the books of Job and Ecclesiastes.

Mesopotamian theology but rather to suggest which ones may have shaped or reflected how the Mesopotamians viewed themselves in relationship to the world around them and especially in connection to their deities. The discussion will focus particularly on what we know about the text so we can determine how widely the ideas in the myth may have been disseminated, who would have known about the text and its contents, how it may have shaped Mesopotamian religious ideas, and how those ideas may have changed over time.

One of the most important religious issues concerns how a group thinks the world was created, its cosmogony. How is the universe constructed and where and how do people fit into it? This is addressed in a number of ancient Mesopotamian myths. While the specific texts may vary in their details, the general idea that humans were created to serve the deities does not change radically.

According to some scholars, the Sumerians addressed cosmogony through a wide variety of textual genres, some particularly specific to the Sumerians. However, no extant Sumerian myths directly address the creation of the world and people's place in it.[16] The most relevant Sumerian mythological texts addressing the origins of the universe and humankind come from the so-called Eridu tradition, with the water-deity Enki as the focus.[17] In *Enki and the World Order, Enki and Ninhursag* (the Dilmun Myth),[18] and *Enki and Ninmah*,[19] the water from Enki's penis waters the world, thereby bringing it to life. Enki does not really create the universe, or himself for that matter, but his emissions bring it to life. Thus, these texts do not really answer the issue of how the earth was formed so much as how it was animated.

Possibly more important in connection with the rest of Mesopotamian tradition is the explanation for humans recounted in *Enki and Ninmah*. While this myth is difficult to understand, and scholars have not agreed on how to translate it, the text begins with the separation of heaven

16. Clifford, *Creation Accounts in the Ancient Near East and in the Bible*, 32. The Sumerian idea of cosmogony is expressed in part through lists and disputations which will be discussed in Chapter 8 below. Note that many scholars consider the disputations to be mythological texts, but they will be treated here as a separate category because they are a fairly unique, creative, intellectual form of philosophical discourse.

17. Clifford, *Creation Accounts*, 13-53.

18. Jacobsen, *The Harps That Once . . .* , 81-204.

19. Klein, "Enki and Ninmah."

and earth. The gods are required to produce their own food, something they do not enjoy, so they complain. Humans are created by adding blood to clay which is then placed inside the womb of the mother-goddess where the new being receives his form and is given birth.[20] Copies of the text date to about 1900-1600 B.C.E., and there even exists a Late Assyrian version with interlinear Babylonian translation.[21] The text therefore has had a long life, suggesting that it was preserved intentionally presumably because some group considered it important.

The theme that mankind was created to do the work for the gods continues through the end of ancient Mesopotamian civilization and in a text more widely promulgated and publicly presented. One of the most famous Mesopotamian mythological texts is *Enuma Elish* ("When on High" in Akkadian, also referred to as the Epic of Creation).[22] This text discusses the origin of the earth, the gods, and the role of humans in the world.

The importance of this text, and thus of the theme imbedded therein, is reinforced in a number of ways. First, *Enuma Elish* served ritual purposes. Several tablets have been preserved which contain major portions of the ritual instruction for the high priest during the New Year festival of Nissanu in Babylon. That text states:

> after the second meal, that of the evening, the high priest of the Etrusha recites from beginning to end (the composition) "When on High" [*Enuma Elish*] to Bel. While he recites the composition "When on High" to Bel, the front of the crown of Anu and the resting place of (the statue of) Enlil are to be covered.[23]

Thus the text was read on a regular basis as part of one of the important cultic festivals in ancient Mesopotamia.[24] This dispels concerns that it was a purely literary composition serving a limited range of people and suggests that the themes inherent in it were at least known to, if not be-

20. Jacobsen, *The Harps That Once . . .* , 151-66. Lambert, "Myth and Mythmaking in Sumer and Akkad," 1833.

21. Lambert, "Myth and Mythmaking," 1833.

22. The text was first made available in Smith, *A Chaldaean Account of Genesis,* and has since been published many times, as recently as the edition by Talon, *The Standard Babylonian Creation Myth.*

23. Cohen, *The Cultic Calendars of the Ancient Near East,* 444.

24. For more about the *Akitu* festival, see Chapter 9 on rituals.

lieved by, a larger population of readers/hearers. Of course, this does not mean that the ritual was the purpose for its composition, only that it represented a later use of the text.[25]

Other evidence supporting the importance of the text is its prevalence in numerous copies and places. Fragments have been found at Nineveh in the library of King Assurbanipal, at the Assyrian city of Assur, at Kish, and at Uruk.[26] While the extant copies reflect different versions (some to be discussed below), there are fewer variants than in many other texts. This lack of variants could mean a number of things. One possibility is that this was a late text and thus there had not been much time for variants to enter the text. Yet because this text appears to have been so well-known and was recited publicly on a yearly basis, it was less likely that changes could creep into it; thus it was almost "canonized."[27] One of the variants is particularly significant: in the Assyrian version the god Assur replaces the Babylonian Marduk as the primary deity who overthrows the older deities. Thus, this myth is not only an example of a text that is not a purely literary creation, but is one that was used in religious ritual and reflects a clear politically motivated theological difference based on place.

Dating *Enuma Elish* is difficult. The text played an important role in the New Year festival, leading many to assume it is an ancient piece of literature, even though the extant copies date to the first millennium. The earliest possible second-millennium date for the text is the reign of Sumu-la-el (1936-1901), the first Amorite ruler of Babylon when Marduk was the patron deity. The Kassite ruler Agum-Kakirme was responsible for returning the cult statue of Marduk to Babylon following the sack of Babylon by the Hittites, and the god's reinstatement in Babylon may have inspired composition of such a text.[28] A lexical list known as An=Anum lists the major gods of the Babylonian pantheon together with their secondary names by assimilation and some of their epithets, and a long section with the names of Marduk includes a subsection that corresponds closely to the names of Marduk appearing on Tablet VII of *Enuma Elish*. A tablet with a list of gods found at the Hittite capital in Anatolia, dating to the second millennium, shows that An = Anum must have included the *Enuma Elish* list of

25. Lambert, "Myth and Mythmaking," 1833.
26. Heidel, *The Babylonian Genesis*, 1.
27. Dalley, *Myths from Mesopotamia*, 229.
28. Dalley, *Myths from Mesopotamia*, 229.

Marduk's names, so some form of the myth must have had a role during the second millennium.[29]

The ritual function of *Enuma Elish* is imbedded in the performance of the New Year festival in Babylon where, as noted, the epic was to be recited (possibly enacted) on the fourth day.[30] The ritual text contains a gap, so it is possible that more than one recital was envisaged. The New Year festival was one of the major religious events of the Mesopotamian calendar.[31] It originally commemorated the god leaving his temporary residence and entering for the first time his permanent home in his chosen city.[32] It later became the ceremony in which the king had his mandate to rule renewed by the gods.[33] *Enuma Elish* celebrated the exaltation of the Babylonian god Marduk (and in Assyria, Assur; see below) and ascribed to Marduk the reorganization of the universe with Babylon in the center, meaning the text was at least at some point used to express Babylonian nationalism.[34] The top officials of the land were called upon to renew their oaths of loyalty to the king and royal family, meaning the ritual reading or enactment would have been known to a broad segment of the population.[35]

The importance of the myth is clear from its content. The text begins, "when skies above were not nor earth below pronounced by name" (Tablet 1:1).[36] Apsu's (male/father)[37] and Tiamat's (female/mother) waters mix together, gods are born in them, and generations of deities follow. In this process, some of the younger gods are already superior to their fathers (1:11-20). The younger gods become too loud and anger Apsu, who calls out to his vizier to join in discussing the issue with Tiamat (1:24-25). Apsu wants to

---

29. Dalley, *Myths from Mesopotamia*, 230.

30. Cohen, *The Cultic Calendars*, 444.

31. See below.

32. Cohen, *The Cultic Calendars*, 405.

33. Dalley, *Myths from Mesopotamia*, 232.

34. Foster, *Before the Muses*, 351.

35. Cohen, *The Cultic Calendars*, 400-53.

36. Translation by Dalley, "Epic of Creation," *Myths from Mesopotamia*, 233-81.

37. The Akkadian term *apsu* means "deep water, sea, cosmic subterranean water, a personified mythological figure, or a water basin in the temple"; *CAD* A II, 194. The Mesopotamians believed springs, wells, streams, rivers, and lakes took water from and were replenished by a freshwater ocean which lay underneath the earth in the *abzu* (*apsu*) or *engur*; Black and Green, "Abzu (apsu)," in *Gods, Demons and Symbols of Ancient Mesopotamia*, 27; Horowitz, *Mesopotamian Cosmic Geography*.

abolish their ways, disperse them, and catch some sleep, but Tiamat will not hear of it and insists he be patient (1:25-47). The vizier sides with Apsu, but the younger gods hear of this; Ea lays out a plan, drenches Apsu with sleep, and slays him (1:46-78). Within Apsu, the god Marduk is created from Ea and Damkina and eventually annoys Tiamat (79-110). The gods turn on Tiamat, who promotes another god, Qingu; she confers upon him leadership of the army and command of the assembly, sets him upon the throne, and gives him the tablet of destinies (1:111-59). Fearing Tiamat, the gods turn to Anu and Ea, who in this case are too afraid and so do nothing (2:5). Ea advises Marduk to take the initiative, to which he agrees, only after laying out the terms by which he will do so; he attacks Tiamat, slays her, and uses her split body to create the heavens (2:127–4:148). Marduk decides to create mankind from Qingu, who they claim had started the war with Tiamat (6:25), so that "the work of the gods shall be imposed (on them) and they [the gods] shall be at leisure" (6:5-8).[38]

Enuma Elish contains material concerning the various deities, how the world was created, and humanity's role in it. The first gods were created from material that preexisted even themselves. The younger deities' overthrowing of the older gods occurs in other polytheistic mythological texts as well and indicates change even within the realm of the gods,[39] a common theme throughout Mesopotamian history. Marduk is almost unknown prior to the first half of the second millennium, and in Assyrian versions of *Enuma Elish* is replaced by the god Assur. Humanity's role in the universe is clear: they were created from the god who began the war between the younger deities and their mother in order that the gods need no longer work. In Assyrian and Babylonian religion, humans were on earth only to serve the deities.

The idea that humans were created so the gods did not have to toil is reinforced, though not the primary focus, in yet another myth, *Atrahasis*,[40] which begins, "When the gods instead of man did the work . . ."[41] Clay tablets with the Old Babylonian version of this myth date to around 1700, and passages of the text appear as late as Assurbanipal's library.[42] Unlike *Enuma*

---

38. The reason for creating man here differs from that of Atrahasis; see below.
39. Graf, "Myth," 48-49.
40. The name means "exceedingly wise."
41. The translation is from Dalley, *Myths from Mesopotamia*, 9.
42. Lambert and Millard, *Atra-Hasis*, 31-39.

Elish, there is no evidence suggesting how this text was used, and it contains no expressed statement of purpose. W. G. Lambert and A. R. Millard suggest that the text gives the impression of having been intended for public recitation, using the Homeric poems as a parallel,[43] and speculate that there may have been an oral tradition alongside the copying of this text.[44] This in no way suggests that the text was clearly well known and broadly disseminated, though the existence of portions spanning a thousand years suggests that some of its basic precepts were known.

In this text, Atrahasis, a citizen of Sharuppak, saves the world from a flood. Humans are created to do the work for the gods, but in this case they are created from a slain god and mixed with clay, and they will hear the drumbeat forever after.[45] After six hundred years the humans become too numerous and, like the gods in *Enuma Elish,* too loud (2:1:1). First the gods send sickness and drought, but that does not work so they come up with a new plan: a flood (2:6:1).[46] Enki warns Atrahasis of the impending deluge and tells him to build a boat and to save living things, not possessions (3:1– end of column). The torrent, storm, and flood last seven days and seven nights. A fifty-eight-line gap follows the reference to the flood, but when the tablets resume someone is sending down food (5:1:1). The gods "gather like flies" over the offering and partake (5:1:5). Now the gods face a dilemma, because they had all agreed to destroy humans but are pleased humans are again cooking for them. They decide there will only be one third as many people, and so create a category of women who will not successfully give birth; there will be a demon among the people who will snatch babies from their mothers' laps; thereby the gods will control childbirth (5:7:1-7).

This myth agrees with *Enuma Elish* and *Enki and Ninmah* that humans are created to provide for the gods, though the process by which it comes about is somewhat different. Here the mother is Mami, but Ea is still involved in their creation. *Atrahasis* also addresses why some women

43. Lambert and Millard, *Atra-Hasis,* 8.
44. Lambert and Millard, *Atra-Hasis,* 31-39.
45. For more on the nature of the noise, see Kilmer, "The Mesopotamian Concept of Overpopulation and Its Solution"; Moran, "Atrahasis."
46. The concept of a world-wide flood, like that in the biblical book of Genesis, appears in Mesopotamian mythological texts and other texts such as the Epic of Gilgamesh, and the Sumerian King List refers to the flood as a historical event. The flood, in Mesopotamian tradition, is not so much a religious concept as a historical event.

do not bear and some children die in childbirth or at a young age. Nevertheless, the similarity to the fundamental concept of humans' role as expressed in the other myths seems to confirm, regardless of the time period, a general religious notion of their purpose on earth.

What happens once humans have fulfilled their primary purpose, or what happens when they die, is addressed in other mythological texts, also with a variety of views. In essence, after death humans go to a netherworld. The text most dedicated to this is *Inanna/Ishtar's Descent to the Netherworld*. This myth is particularly useful when discussing Mesopotamian religion as a larger category, rather than simply Sumerian or Babylonian, because it is one of the few mythological texts that had a clear Sumerian prototype. It is also a rare case where the Sumerian version is fuller than the later Akkadian. (The complicated issue of the relationship between Sumerian Inanna and Akkadian Ishtar will be considered in Chapter 5 on the deities.)

The Sumerian text of *Inanna's Descent to the Netherworld* is reconstructed from thirteen tablets, all excavated at Nippur. All of the tablets were inscribed in the first half of the second millennium, but their original date of composition is not known and there are no third-millennium exemplars.[47] The fact that the text, which was found at only one site, was copied in Sumerian means that it was considered an important part of Sumerian literature that needed to be preserved. As noted, the Sumerian text is fuller, and it explains the association to Dumuzi/Tammuz in a way the Akkadian version does not.[48] The existence of an Akkadian version, regardless of the similarities or differences, suggests a continuity with main themes in Mesopotamian religion.

The text begins with a list of the seven important cities which had temples to Inanna,[49] but it does not indicate why they are named. The text also reports that Inanna takes the seven *mes* with her to the Netherworld.[50] Translating the Sumerian word *me* is difficult. It is a plural, inanimate noun and refers to properties or powers of the gods which enable a whole

47. Kramer, "Sumerian Myths and Epic Tales," 52.

48. Kramer, "Inanna's Descent to the Nether World"; "The Third Tablet of the Ur Version."

49. Kramer, "Sumerian Myths and Epic Tales," 52.

50. The primary source of information about the *mes* is from another myth, "Inanna and Enki: The Transfer of the Arts of Civilization from Eridu to Erech"; Kramer, *The Sumerians*, 160-62.

host of activities essential for civilized human life to take place.[51] Thus, Inanna's abandoning her cities and leaving with what some call the "arts of civilization" cannot be good. Inanna then clothes herself with a variety of jewels and even applies her make-up. Next she tells her messenger that she is going to the Netherworld and instructs him on what to do, implying that she knows she will have trouble coming back. The messenger is to tell Enlil what has happened to his daughter and not to let her be put to death in the Netherworld.

When Inanna arrives at the lapis lazuli palace of the Netherworld, she tells the gatekeeper to open the house. When asked why, Inanna responds that she is going to visit her sister Ereshkigal, whose husband, the Lord Gugalanna, has been killed and that she intends to attend his funeral rites. She is instructed to disrobe because the ordinances of the Netherworld are perfect. Inanna is apparently turned into a corpse, and her messenger carries out the original task she had ordered.

The messenger first goes to the E-kur (Enlil's temple) in Ur. Enlil suggests that Inanna has reaped what she herself had requested, so he is not inclined to help. Then the messenger goes to Nanna, also in Ur, who replies the same as Enlil. The messenger also goes to Eridu, to Enki, who is troubled. From the dirt under his nail Enki fashions the food and water of life. The water is sprinkled on Inanna, and she ascends from the Netherworld, followed by the *annunaki,* and the dead hasten in front of her. Inanna is told she must be replaced in the Netherworld by someone. When she finds her husband, Dumuzi/Tammuz, having a party while she was in the Netherworld, she decides to send him to take her place. For reasons explained in a break in the text, Dumuzi's sister appears to go to the Netherworld part of the year in his place.

The Akkadian version clearly has enough similarities to show that the accounts are related, yet it differs in a number of substantial ways. The text is preserved in two manuscripts discovered from Assurbanipal's library and an earlier variant version recovered from Assur.[52] In this text, Ishtar, who in her Akkadian permutation is often described as a goddess of love and war but possibly better described as the goddess of adrenaline,[53] de-

---

51. Black and Green, "Me," in *Gods, Demons and Symbols,* 130.

52. Foster, *Before the Muses,* 403

53. The reason for this statement is more obvious in Chapter 5 below, in the discussion of Inanna/Ishtar.

cides to go to the Netherworld, the land of her sister Ereshkigal (1:1).[54] The text provides no reason why she should go. The Netherworld is described as a "dark house," on the road that is "one-way only," where "those who enter are deprived of light," "dirt is their food, clay their bread," and they "live in darkness" and are "clothed like birds, with feathers" (1:5-10). The door to the place is bolted, and dust has settled upon the bolt (11).

Ishtar demands of the gatekeeper he let her in, and if he does not she will smash the door, shatter the bolt, and "raise up the dead and they shall eat the living so that the dead shall outnumber the living" (1:19). The gatekeeper warns Ereshkigal, who wonders what her sister wants (25-31). Ereshkigal's self-described job is to eat clay for bread, drink muddy water for beer, and weep for young men forced to abandon sweethearts, girls wrenched from their lovers' laps, and the infant child expelled before its time (32-36).

Ereshkigal instructs the gatekeeper to open his gate to Ishtar, but to treat her according to the ancient rites (37-38). This will involve taking Ishtar through seven different doors, each time stripping her of an article of jewelry, including the great crown on her head, the rings in her ears, the beads around her neck, the toggle pins at her breast, the girdle of birthstones around her waist, the bangles on her wrists and ankles, and the proud garment of her body (40-62).

The problem with Ishtar's presence in the Netherworld is that while she is away from home, "no bull mounted a cow [no donkey impregnated a jenny], no young man impregnated a girl . . ." (86-89). Ishtar's absence, or rather her presence, naked, in the Netherworld keeps the other world from creating new life. This causes dejection among the great gods until Ea creates a good-looking playboy to cheer up Ereshkigal (91-99). When he asks for water Ereshkigal becomes angry, but somehow Ishtar is sprinkled with the waters of life and leaves through each door, receiving all the jewels originally taken from her (1:100-30). The Akkadian version ends with a reference to "the day when Dumuzi comes back up" (136). Unlike the Sumerian version, according to which food and water are smuggled to Inanna, she is told she must be replaced in the Netherworld by someone, finds her husband Dumuzi/Tammuz feasting in her absence and so decides to send

54. In another text, "How Nergal Became the King of the Netherworld," Ereshkigal takes a lover who also becomes king of the Netherworld; Foster, *From Distant Days*, 85-96.

him to take her place, and his sister appears to go to the Netherworld part of the year for him; none of this is recorded in the Akkadian version.

The variations between the two texts speak both to differences between the Sumerian Inanna and Akkadian Ishtar and to the point of the myth, at least as far as shedding light on Mesopotamian religion. There has been much discussion about the relationship between the texts, including why Inanna/Ishtar goes down in the first place and how she is saved. The Sumerian text attempts to connect Inanna with her cities and some of her powers, while there is no such effort in the Ishtar version. In the Sumerian, Inanna makes a pretense at having reason to go down, and some would suggest it is to seize power over the Netherworld, whereas Ishtar just demands it. Possibly most significantly, in the Sumerian Inanna has to tell someone what is going to happen to her so she can be rescued, whereas the world undergoes significant change when Ishtar disappears. In both cases the text is fairly entertaining, with a great deal of sexual innuendo and drama.[55] Are the differences then suggestive of changing religious sensibilities or simply indicating a focus on entertainment?

Regardless of whether the text was intended for entertainment or deep philosophical reflection, it describes the Netherworld as a place where people go after life. Though not described in great detail, the concept is not challenged significantly in other texts. The Netherworld is a one-way ticket. Once one enters one cannot, with the exception of Ishtar and her replacement, return to life above. The place is dark, and the food and beer are not good. The people there range from babies who die too young, to lovers separated. Ereshkigal, who controls that realm, claims the task of weeping over them all. Thus the reality of death is existence in some other, unpleasant, state, from which there is no return. Ereshkigal highlights the dark side of the issue, yet simultaneously expresses tenderness and caring for her charges. The darkness of the Netherworld emphasizes the good things to be found before death: good food, beer, love, and light.

Conclusions

These are not the only mythological texts with religious themes, nor is this the only genre of texts shedding light on Mesopotamian religion. As noted

---

55. Jacobsen, *The Harps that Once . . .* , 205.

above, the myths are discussed separately here precisely because whether these texts contain any kind of religious doctrine, are for ritual purposes, or are for pure entertainment is not clear. These are not the only issues raised by mythological texts. Other themes include the destiny of the order of civilization,[56] human mortality,[57] and childlessness.[58] What is important for the texts treated thus far is their focus on a main theological premise for Mesopotamians: the world was controlled by a series of deities who invented humans so that they did not have to work. Questions concerning who the deities were, which ones were the most important, and how humans were supposed to worship (take care of) them will be discussed in the following chapters.

56. The Myth of Zu, translated in *ANET,* 111-13, 514-17; or "Anzu," in Dalley, *Myths from Mesopotamia.* For a full treatment of the text, see Annus, *The Standard Babylonian Epic of Anzu.*

57. "Adapa," *ANET,* 101; and Dalley, *Myths from Mesopotamia,* 182-88. For a fuller discussion, see Izre'el, *Adapa and the South Wind.*

58. Addressed in Atrahasis and the Etana Epic.

CHAPTER 5

The Gods

A s with all things Mesopotamian, it is not possible in this introductory volume to provide a full overview of all the gods, their functions, and how they were viewed by the Mesopotamians. Instead, the effort will be to provide an account of the history of what we know about the Mesopotamian pantheon in general and how it evolved. This chapter will provide a brief overview of the kinds of deities there were and how some of them evolved over time and place. In this way, the reader can see the issues involved in trying to understand the role the deities played in the various places and periods under discussion.

The Mesopotamian Pantheon

The Mesopotamian pantheon is complex because, like all of Mesopotamian civilization, it exhibits change and continuity. The various deities appear in mythological texts, but they are defined in other texts as well: legal, literary, historical, and ritual.[1] Depictions of the gods and their symbols appear in seals, sealings, wall carvings, and statuary, though no ancient Mesopotamian cult statue has yet been excavated. Because the data concerning the gods span close to two thousand years, a number of inconsistencies appear, which is problematic for scholars trying to understand how the Mesopotamians constructed their world and religious system. Yet,

---

1. See Chapter 8 below on "Religious Texts."

there is no more confusion in the ancient world as to who the deities were, how they functioned, or humans' relationship to them than is expressed in such biblical books as Job or Ecclesiastes.

In reference to Egypt, David Silverman comments,

> some scholars think it futile to try to organize the gods of Egypt into groups. First, it can be argued that any such effort results in a structure that is the product of a modern mind, not an ancient one. Second, proposed groupings result in so much overlapping that the boundaries of the categories dissolve. The multiple roles of certain divinities allow some of them to function in more than one grouping at a time and some deities appear in a particular classification during one period but not during another.[2]

A similar concern is expressed by Jeremy Black and Anthony Green when they suggest,

> There is a sense in which it is impossible, in connection with ancient Mesopotamia, to speak of a pantheon[3] ("the deities of a people collectively"). This is because under the (geographically ill-determined) heading Mesopotamia, at least 3,000 years of history are included, incorporating three main peoples (Sumerians, Babylonians and Assyrians).[4]

Black and Green also note that there is no collective or authoritative statement of all Mesopotamian myths involving deities, as is the case for Classical Greece in Hesiod's *Theogony* or Ovid's *Metamorphoses*. Furthermore, there are numerous gods and types of gods whose tasks change with time, place, circumstance, and type of text referring to them. Yet unlike the Egyptians, the ancient Mesopotamians did keep lists of their deities, though there is debate about what those lists mean and how they should be evaluated.[5]

From the time of the Sumerians through the first millennium B.C.E.,

---

2. Silverman, "Divinity and Deities in Ancient Egypt," 30-32.

3. A pantheon is generally defined as "all the gods of a people"; *Webster's New World Dictionary: Second Collegiate Edition* (1986), 1026.

4. Black and Green, *Gods, Demons and Symbols*, 147.

5. See Chapter 8 below on "Religious Texts."

Votive statue of Puzur-Ishtar, Governor of Mari, 1950 B.C.E.
(Pergamon Museum, Berlin; photo by Susanne Pratscher)

the Mesopotamians kept lists[6] that address everything from professions, to things made of metal, to gods. The god lists are some of the earliest Sumerian documents and include as many as 560 names of deities.[7] Another list, An=Anum, dating to the middle of the second millennium, includes approximately two thousand names, though the order here is not identical to that of the earlier Sumerian lists; instead, it groups the deities according to families.[8] The Assyrian kings at the end of the second and beginning of

6. Oppenheim, *Ancient Mesopotamia*, 244-48.

7. Krebernik, "Die Götterlisten aus Faran"; Mander, *Il Pantheon di Abu-Sālabīkh*.

8. Litke, *A Reconstruction of the Assyro-Babylonian God-Lists AN:dAnu-um and AN:Anu ša amēli*.

the first millennium wrote "annals,"[9] and starting with Tiglath-pileser I (1114-1076) these annals open with a list of deities.[10] Not all the gods appear at the beginning of these texts, and different versions of annals within one Assyrian king's reign may include different deities in this section of the text; but they always follow the same order as those represented in the earliest god lists.[11] Thus, though the list of deities may change, something about their order defies modification. This also indicates some structure and organizing principle to the pantheon that the Sumerians suggested, difficult as it may be for modern scholars to discern.

Mesopotamia abounded with many gods and varieties of deities.[12] Most famous were those of the main pantheon, to whom all owed some form of allegiance. Each city was responsible for one or more deities, and personal deities served to help a particular family connect with the larger pantheon and to work on their behalf.[13]

History and Evolution of the Pantheon

Scholars have identified a general pattern marked by three to four stages in the history of the pantheon in Mesopotamia. In general, these stages are associated with political and population shifts in the region, even, some argue, directly connected to the fortunes of the gods' priestly counterparts on earth.[14] The early phase begins in the fourth millennium B.C.E. and centers on worship of powers in nature and other phenomena related to basic survival. In the second stage, dating to the third millennium, rulers were deified and the pantheon became more structured. The next stage dates to the second millennium, with greater emphasis on individuals and common folks as seen in the greater role played by personal gods. The final stage is rooted in the political formation of empire, and

9. Grayson, "Assyria and Babylonia."

10. Rawlinson, *A Selection from the Historical Inscriptions of Chaldaea, Assyria, and Babylonia;* Grayson, *Assyrian Royal Inscriptions* 2.

11. Schneider, *A New Analysis of the Royal Annals of Shalmaneser III,* 44-52.

12. The total number of Mesopotamian deities has been variously figured, from 2,400 (Tallqvist, *Akkadische Götterepitheta*) to as high as 3,300 (Deimel, *Pantheon babylonicum*).

13. See below.

14. Hallo and van Dijk, *The Exaltation of Inanna,* 6.

the number of deities appears to shrink with more power concentrated on fewer deities.[15]

Many of the deities were originally associated with elements of nature and then transferred to areas of human civilization at a later period. For example, the Sumerian Utu (Semitic Shamash) probably originated as the sun-god, but since the sun sees everything he became the god of justice as well.[16] Sumerian Enki (Semitic Ea) was the god of the subterranean freshwater ocean, the clever god, and by extension the friend of humans.[17] Sumerian Ishkur (Semitic Adad) had a similar role among peoples in many areas adjacent to Assyria and Babylonia, such as the Hurrians and Hittites. He began as the god of the wind or storm, but also was a foundation for centralized political power.[18] When the gods are depicted, their attributes, and to some extent their original element of nature, are shown flowing from their shoulders. For example, rays emanate from Shamash,[19] water from Ea,[20] and lightning or flowing streams from Adad.[21]

In the earlier periods, numerous deities, especially females, functioned in regard to various aspects of fertility. As Black and Green point out, in popular writing about polytheistic, especially premodern religions, the term "mother goddess" is widely used with a fairly large range of meaning. They note that for historical periods in Mesopotamia we have definite information about mother and birth goddesses.[22] In the third millennium motherhood of most of the early gods was ascribed to one particular goddess, who by the second millennium B.C.E. appears under a variety of interchangeable names, some of which become titles.[23] Nammu, Ninhur-

15. Jacobsen, *The Treasures of Darkness*, 21. For Jacobsen, this period embodies a "barbarization" of the idea of divinity and is identified with "narrow national political aspirations," so he does not regard it as a category like the other periods and treats it only as an epilogue for contrast. This probably highlights more about Jacobsen's understanding of "religion" than anything regarding Mesopotamia.

16. Black and Green, *Gods, Demons and Symbols*, 182-84.

17. Black and Green, *Gods, Demons and Symbols*, 75.

18. Green, *The Storm-God in the Ancient Near East*, 281; Frymer-Kensky, *In the Wake of the Goddesses*.

19. Black and Green, *Gods, Demons and Symbols*, 183-84.

20. Black and Green, *Gods, Demons and Symbols*, 75.

21. Black and Green, *Gods, Demons and Symbols*, 111.

22. Black and Green, *Gods, Demons and Symbols*, 132.

23. Black and Green, *Gods, Demons and Symbols*, 132.

saga, and Ninlil (Mullissa) were all "mother goddesses" who did not survive into Semitic permutations without serious changes. Ninmah served more the role of a midwife than a mother goddess; nevertheless she is almost identical with Ninhursaga and the focus on reproduction and fertility remains intact.[24]

Possibly because the type of data available in the second or third stage of development of the Mesopotamian pantheon is more text-focused than for the earlier periods, we note the appearance of a group of deities[25] more connected with "arts of civilization." While it may appear odd to modern readers, the Mesopotamians had separate deities for such diverse and important components of society as beer and beer-making (Ninkasi),[26] healing (Gula),[27] and writing (Nabu).[28] Some of these types of deities were worshipped in a particular city; however, because the focus of their expertise addresses specific occupations, they transcend city location for a select group of the population.

The unique features of these deities provide interesting shifts in their personas. For example, Gula, "who understands disease," had her principal shrine in the city of Isin but also had temples at Nippur, Borsippa, and Assur. By extension of her area of expertise, healing, she was also a patroness of doctors.[29] Nabu was the divine god of destinies. His association with writing allowed him to be joined later with Enki and Marduk as a god of wisdom, though in other traditions he absorbed attributes of Ninurta and was associated with irrigation and agriculture. In fact, the worship of this deity may have actually come to Mesopotamia from Syria. His cult center became Borsippa.[30]

Nabu also serves as a good example of what happened with some deities in the final stage of the Mesopotamian pantheon's development, the period of empire. Apparently, as a result of the combination of the prox-

24. Black and Green, *Gods, Demons and Symbols,* 135, 140-41.

25. Here I am only vaguely grouping them in this way to highlight the slightly different type of issues associated with these deities. I am not claiming they are a group defined by the ancient Mesopotamians or even modern scholarship.

26. Beer, following Mesopotamian recipes, has been made recently by Anchor Steam Brewing Company; see www.anchorbrewing.com/beers/ninkasi.htm.

27. Black and Green, "Gula," *Gods, Demons and Symbols,* 101.

28. Black and Green, "Nabu," *Gods, Demons and Symbols,* 133-34.

29. Black and Green, "Gula," *Gods, Demons and Symbols,* 101.

30. Black and Green, "Nabu," *Gods, Demons and Symbols,* 133-34.

imity of Borsippa to Babylon along with Nabu's role in wisdom, he was absorbed into the circle of the god Marduk, first as his minister and later (in the Kassite period) as his son. Nabu finally became the supreme god of Babylonia alongside Marduk.[31] Thus, even the deities who did not begin as nature deities followed a fairly complicated path.

Major Deities

The influence of individual Mesopotamian deities changed over time and place, as do the available sources referring to them. While the evolution of less important deities reflects these changes, those most prominent in the hierarchy at times show even more substantially the impact of political trends in the area. We will examine here the two deities who head the god list, as well as Ishtar and the two titular deities of Babylonia and Assyria. These five major deities are representative of the issues affecting the pantheon and are illustrative of deities who appear in a number of media, and their personas reflect the fluctuations in the history and religious status of the region.

The first name on the god list from Sharrupak and Abu Salibikh is An. The name An is the Sumerian word for "heaven" and also the name of the god called the "sky-god."[32] An appears in the semi-pictographic economic texts from Jemdet Nasr,[33] though it is difficult to ascertain whether he is mentioned as the recipient of offerings.[34] The texts from the Sumerian period delineate three main functions for An: universal god of creation, inhabitant of heaven, and bestower of the royal insignia (founder of earthly royal power), but much of that had changed by the time Babylon and Assur gained prominence.[35]

An was considered the prime deity involved in creation and leader of the gods, but by the time of *Enuma Elish* he had yielded his place of primacy to Marduk. A transition of sorts had begun already by the end of the third millennium; by the reign of Gudea (ca. 2200-2100), An and Enlil ap-

31. Black and Green, "Nabu," *Gods, Demons and Symbols,* 133-34.
32. *CAD* A II, 146.
33. Wohlstein, *The Sky-God An-Anu.*
34. Wohlstein, *The Sky-God An-Anu,* 29.
35. Wohlstein, *The Sky-God An-Anu,* 25.

pear in parallel positions,[36] though at the end of the Ur III period (ca. 2006) An was still king of the gods.[37] It is really only in the Old Babylonian period where significant shifts occurred. Official royal inscriptions and date-lists have An appearing alongside Enlil, but data provided by proper names show An receding behind the local veneration of the other deities, especially Marduk and Shamash.[38]

An's position at the head of the pantheon for such a long period suggests that he should be a deity well involved in the human world, yet his actual role was almost nonexistent in the religious life of Mesopotamia. His nature and attributes are ill-defined and so he is rarely represented in art and iconography.[39]

Enlil is the second major deity on the list and also is considered the king of the gods. His role stems from being the offspring of An (Enuma Elish), though he is also described as a descendant of Enki and Ninki.[40] Enlil's supreme position as ruler of the universe and controller of the affairs of humans and gods was guaranteed through his possession of the tablet of destinies (the mes) and his crown and throne.[41]

Enlil's primary residence was the ancient Sumerian city of Nippur, which may account for the trajectory of his role throughout Mesopotamian history. Nippur had become the religious capital of the alluvial plain by 2700, and as long as Enlil reigned as king of the gods, his city received the veneration of the inhabitants. By the middle of the twenty-fourth century, a king's control of Nippur, and therefore claim to Enlil's choosing him for kingship, provided a divine basis for his authority.[42] This is precisely when An's power had begun to wane, as seen in the inscriptions where both An and Enlil are treated together.[43] Enlil's role continued even in the transition from the period of Sumerian hegemony to the first reign of an Amorite ruler, apparent when Ishbi-Irra proclaimed himself king in

36. Wohlstein, *The Sky-God An-Anu*, 35-36.

37. Wohlstein, *The Sky-God An-Anu*, 44.

38. Wohlstein, *The Sky-God An-Anu*, 84.

39. Black and Green, "An (Anu)," *Gods, Demons and Symbols*, 30.

40. Black and Green, "Enlil," *Gods, Demons and Symbols*, 76.

41. Black and Green, "Tablets of Destinies," *Gods, Demons and Symbols*, 173. The tablet of destinies invested its holder with the power to determine the fate of the world.

42. For a thorough analysis of Nippur, see Cole, *Nippur in Late Assyrian Times c. 755-612*.

43. Wohlstein, *The Sky-God An-Anu*, 35-36.

Isin, saying, "Enlil . . . has given the kingship to Ishbi-Irra, who is not of the seed of Sumer."[44]

Enlil and Nippur's status declined considerably when Hammurabi and his successors dominated the region.[45] There was a revival of Nippur's fortune during the Kassite period until shortly after 1230 B.C.E., when the king of Elam attacked the city and scattered the people.[46] Approximately one hundred years after the onset of Nippur's decline, Enlil handed his kingship over the gods to Marduk of Babylon.[47] Slightly before Enlil's strength waned in Babylon and he was replaced by Marduk, in Assyria there are traces of attempts to identify Assur with him.[48] At this time, Assur was assimilating major deities from the Sumerian and Babylonian pantheon, whereas Marduk replaced them in Babylonia.

Inanna is considered to be represented in the Akkadian world as Ishtar, though there are personality shifts in the transition. Understanding Inanna/Ishtar is complicated by both the ancient texts and modern notions of the role of women in society, both ancient and modern. Cuneiform literature variously describes her as the daughter of An, the moon-god Sin (Sumerian Nanna), Enlil, or even Enki. Her siblings include her brother, the sun-god Shamash (Sumerian Utu). and her sister, queen of the Netherworld Ereshkigal.[49] While there was in general a diminution of goddesses from the Sumerian period throughout the Old Babylonian period and later, with fewer stories about female deities, Ishtar grew in importance.[50] Inanna/Ishtar's persona has three main components: the goddess of love and sexual behavior, a warlike goddess who is fond of battle, and the planet Venus, the morning and evening star.[51]

Sumerian Inanna is difficult to separate from the Akkadian Ishtar because the two were linked somewhat early in Mesopotamian history, and

44. Cole, *Nippur in Late Assyrian Times*, 9.

45. There was a change in the course of the Euphrates River, and it is not clear if this happened because of natural causes or human manipulation; Cole, *Nippur in Late Assyrian Times*, 10-11.

46. Cole, *Nippur in Late Assyrian Times*, 12; Grayson, *Assyrian and Babylonian Chronicles*, 176, tablet iv 15.

47. Cole, *Nippur in Late Assyrian Times*, 12.

48. Black and Green, "Assur," *Gods, Demons and Symbols*, 38.

49. Black and Green, *Gods, Demons and Symbols*, 108-9.

50. Frymer-Kensky, *In the Wake of the Goddesses*, 71-77.

51. Black and Green, *Gods, Demons and Symbols*, 109.

the connection appears to be intentional and political.[52] Sargon, as noted earlier, was the first to unite Mesopotamia, and he shifted the bureaucratic language from Sumerian to Akkadian. He also established his daughter, Enheduanna, as the priestess of the moon-god, Nanna/Sin, in Ur. Some suggest that Sargon's connection to and the importance he placed on cultic matters lie behind the legend that he himself was the product of a union between a high priestess and some unknown father. In the historical tradition Sargon is variously the son, lover, or father of a priestess representing the goddess.[53]

The question here is how Enheduanna, priestess of Nanna, affected Inanna and Ishtar. While most texts from ancient Mesopotamia are anonymous, Enheduanna is named the author of a number of works. In one of her texts, she is expelled from both Ur and Uruk, the seats of Nanna and An, the god of heaven. It is Nanna's daughter Inanna who restored her and to whom Enheduanna dedicated a hymn.[54] William Hallo and J. J. A. van Dijk argue that Sargon, in a conscious effort to replace the loose alliance of Sumer and Akkad with a centralized system, modified the cultic and dynastic institutions of the south to his own purposes by instituting a cultic union of the chief priestly offices in the person of his daughter Enheduanna, a devotee of Inanna. He equated the Sumerian Inanna with the Akkadian Ishtar to lay the theological foundations for a united empire of Sumer and Akkad.[55] If this theory is correct, it would suggest that the association of the Sumerian deities with the Akkadian-named deities was not a natural shift but a conscious and politically-motivated action, at least in this case.

While Sargon may have intentionally modified who and what Inanna was or represented, he could not have made the connection between Inanna and Ishtar, nor could any of the other associations be made if some of the pieces were not already in place. This again raises the issue of the nature of polytheistic thought and worldview. Though the deities are clearly differentiated and personalized by name, shape, and function, there is also a semantic commonality that facilitates translations of the names and allows for gods from different cultures or parts of a culture to be equated.

52. Hallo and van Dijk, *The Exaltation of Inanna*, 6.
53. Hallo and van Dijk, *The Exaltation of Inanna*, 6-7.
54. Hallo and van Dijk, *The Exaltation of Inanna*, 8-9.
55. Hallo and van Dijk, *The Exaltation of Inanna*, 9.

Numerous Sumerian-Akkadian glossaries have been excavated, including lists of divine names in two or even three languages.[56] This helps to explain not only how Sargon may have managed his theological coup but also how these and other deities shifted over time.

Further confusion surrounding Inanna/Ishtar's role in society stems from the various texts in which she appears. When she goes down to the Netherworld in the "Descent of Ishtar to the Netherworld," sexuality on earth ceases. She is married, but in the Epic of Gilgamesh, Gilgamesh refers to her past lovers as a reason not to marry her.[57] She has no children, so her importance for repopulation is not in the act of reproduction but for creating in people and animals the desire to cohabit. She is well known also as goddess of war and for others' interest in taking her into battle.[58] In the Sacred Marriage, a rite for which literary evidence dates only to the Sumerian period, a human priestess representing Inanna marries the king.[59] It is not clear if this was an actual occurrence or a ritual enactment, but if Inanna and Ishtar are equated, this links Ishtar closely with the king's legitimacy to rule.[60]

Recent scholarship has shown that sexuality and sexual excitement are not necessarily related to love, as is especially clear in rape, which is more about aggression and dominance than sexuality.[61] The connection between dominance and excitement in Ishtar's case may hold the key to understanding her. Ishtar's interest is in sexuality, not marriage, either for herself or others. What drives her is adrenaline and excitement, a link to her role as "mistress of battle and war" and evidenced by some of her attributes: fierce in terror, exalted (in) the awesome strength of a young bull, able to turn man to woman and woman to man.[62]

---

56. Assman, "Monotheism and Polytheism," 24.

57. Tablet VI, obv. col. i-iii. Gilgamesh lists her lovers, all of whom met negative fates.

58. See her "self-praise" in Foster, *Before the Muses,* 1:74.

59. Black and Green, *Gods, Demons and Symbols,* 158. For more on the "Sacred Marriage," see Chapter 9 on "Rituals."

60. Frymer-Kensky, *In the Wake of the Goddesses,* 58. For a thorough and detailed analysis of the Sumerian Sacred Marriage in all of its manifestations, see Lapinkivi, *The Sumerian Sacred Marriage.*

61. Yee, *Poor Banished Children of Eve.*

62. These traits are all mentioned in "Ishtar, Queen of Heaven" (translation in Foster, *Before the Muses,* 2:501-7), which Lambert has shown is a conflation and rework-

The supreme national deities of the Assyrians and Babylonians do not follow the same trajectory as those who dominated the Sumerian pantheon but who then declined or shifted in power. Assur and Marduk were relatively unknown in the third millennium. Like other Mesopotamian gods, they were linked to specific cities, but their role developed differently because of the power those cities would later gain. These deities further gained power from the other deities and each other. Thus, the final stage of the Mesopotamian pantheon builds off of traditions already well established by the time they become dominant in the first millennium.

Marduk was the patron deity of Babylon and is known as early as the Early Dynastic period.[63] His real power came through the political and subsequent cultural rise of the city of Babylon following the reign of Hammurabi. *Enuma Elish* addresses this development on the cosmic level, but the politics behind the shift towards Marduk's ascent are noted in the Code of Hammurabi, where An and Enlil name the city but give supreme authority to Marduk.[64] Because of this close tie between the political and cultural influence of Babylon and the deity, Marduk's absence, usually because of war and the destruction of the city, demanded explanation in the both the political and religious realms. Numerous literary texts depict the disaster that ensued whenever Marduk left Babylon,[65] usually portraying him as having abandoned the city.[66] Just as Babylon gained sway over Mesopotamia, its deity also gained supremacy in the pantheon, and the city itself increased in status as the most important religious center in Mesopotamia.

The conflict between Babylonia and Assyria and Babylon's cultural dominance are reflected in the depiction of each region's titular deity. Assur was the deity of the Assyrians and probably originated as the local deity of the city Assur. Around 1300 B.C.E., he began to be identified with Sumerian Enlil, chief of the gods.[67] When Tukulti-Ninurta I defeated the

---

ing of various texts about Ishtar. The last attribute refers to sexual deviation, one of her domains.

63. Black and Green, "Marduk," *Gods, Demons and Symbols,* 128.

64. Laws of Hammurabi, Prologue line 7.

65. A number of texts poetically recount events concerning Marduk's departure and return, e.g., "Agum-Kakirme and the Return of Marduk" (Foster, *Before the Muses,* 1:274-77); "The War with Elam" (294-95); "The Return of Marduk from Elam" (299-300); "Nebuchadnezzar and Marduk" (301); "Nebuchadnezzar to the Babylonians" (302); and "Marduk Prophecy" (304-7).

66. Van de Mieroop, *The Ancient Mesopotamian City,* 48.

Babylonian Kassite king Kashtiliash IV, he brought back the statue of Marduk. Though the Assyrians assumed responsibility to maintain the cult of the captured Marduk, the historical background was reinterpreted and Assur replaced Marduk as the chief deity honored during the Akītu festival, including the trial of Marduk for transgressions against Assur.[68] As Assyria grew in military and political power, so too did their deity. When the Assyrian kings moved their capital to Calah (Nimrud) and then Nineveh, Assur maintained his status as deity of the expanded state.[69]

This brief overview of some of the major deities of the Mesopotamian pantheon highlights the direct connection between the role of a deity and its titular city. The level of intentionality behind the politics of the rise and fall of different gods is difficult to ascertain. Did the kings, priests, or scribes intentionally shape texts to emphasize their deity's power so the people would follow that deity, or did they believe the deity achieved prominence thus making possible the creation of new and modification of old stories and treatments of the gods? Did the "common" people follow these varying traditions, or are the textual references to the gods and their change of rank intended solely for the elite? These questions are complicated by the difficulty of dating texts or determining their earliest composition.

Personal Gods

Most of the literary legacy from Mesopotamia reflects the perspective or situation of the upper echelon of society, consisting mostly of royalty, scribes, and priesthood. Among the rest of society, personal gods played a major role. These deities, like the individuals for whom they intervened, were not a component of the power structure, earthly or divine.

As with the other deities, the personal gods also change with time and, to some extent, follow the pattern seen with the stages of development of the Mesopotamian pantheon. Because personal gods are rarely named and

67. Black and Green, *Gods, Demons and Symbols,* 38.

68. Cohen, *The Cultic Calendars of the Ancient Near East,* 422. For further discussion, see Chapter 9 on "Rituals."

69. For a detailed discussion of how the Assyrian kings incorporated religion with their political powers, see Holloway, *Assur Is King! Assur Is King!*

we would have no indication or representation of them in the earliest stages, they are largely unattested. In the mid-third millennium, some rulers regarded a particular deity or deities as being in some intimate way their special protector. Sargon and the kings of his dynasty appear to have a special allegiance to Illaba, and Gudea addresses the goddess Gatumdug as "mother and father," while Utu-hegal asks Dumuzi and Gilgamesh to be his "protectors."[70] All of these patrons are royalty and name the specific deities, so it is not clear if this reflects the same phenomena that became more prominent in the second millennium.

In the second millennium, the personal gods appear to function more on behalf of common persons. A number of texts indicate that the gods came to be increasingly identified with political ambitions,[71] especially as evidenced with the rise of Marduk and later Assur. In fact, for Thorkild Jacobsen, the appearance of the personal god is the hallmark of the pantheon in this stage. The function of the personal gods was to see that their client's situation received attention by taking his or her case to the greater gods.[72] The deity is usually named and is referred to by the worshipper as "my god" or "my goddess."[73]

Omens, wisdom literature, and personal prayers offer insight into the role of personal gods. One tablet suggests their protective capacity: "One who has no god, as he walks along the street, Headache [a disease demon] envelops him like a garment."[74] Luck and good fortune are described as "acquiring a god." In the omen literature, a favorable portent may indicate "that house will acquire a god, that house will endure," and the reverse, a bad portent, indicates "that house will grow poor, will not acquire a god."[75] The drama of humans' relationship to these gods is evident in texts such as "A Man and His God," in which a man complains directly to his personal god when he appears to have no luck.[76] Some texts provide instructions of how to address the personal gods:

70. Black and Green, *Gods, Demons and Symbols,* 148. See also Chapter 10 below on "Kingship, Religion, and the Gods."

71. Nemet-Nejat, *Daily Life in Ancient Mesopotamia,* 180.

72. Lambert, *Babylonian Wisdom Literature,* 7.

73. Black and Green, *Gods, Demons and Symbols,* 148.

74. Lambert, *Babylonian Wisdom Literature,* 7.

75. Jacobsen, *The Treasures of Darkness,* 155.

76. Foster, *Before the Muses,* 2:640-43, and Lambert, "DINGIR SA.DIB2.BA Incantations."

Every day worship your god. Sacrifice and benediction are the proper accompaniment of incense. Present your free-will offering to your god, for this is proper toward the gods. Prayer, supplication and prostration offer him daily and you will get your reward. Then you will have full communion with your god.[77]

The "Babylonian Theodicy," an acrostic poem in the form of a dialogue between a sufferer and a friend, sums up the Mesopotamian understanding of the world in which they lived based on the nature of the relationship between humans and the various divinities. The sufferer exposes the evils of current social injustice, while the friend tries to reconcile these facts with established views of justice and the divine ordering of the universe. Both sufferer and friend begin with the premise that the gods are responsible for maintaining justice among humans, yet end by admitting these very gods make humans prone to injustice.[78]

Conclusions

Reflecting on the pantheon of Mesopotamian deities reveals that the sufferer in the above text may have had it right. In the Mesopotamian world, the deities, their roles, functions, and status change with the fortunes of the different cities, regions, politicians, and priests. While it is not clear whether all of these modifications to the identity of deities and what they represented were intentional or not, the nature of polytheistic religion allowed for such shifts to be easily accepted, or at least incorporated, into the textual religious tradition of the region. It was, therefore, the scribes who determined who and what the Mesopotamian deities were and thereby, as the sufferer suggests, held them responsible for making humans prone to injustice.

77. Lambert, *Babylonian Wisdom Literature,* 105, lines 135-40.
78. Lambert, *Babylonian Wisdom Literature,* 65.

CHAPTER 6

The Temples

A Mesopotamian temple served as the home of a particular deity. Since humans were on earth to serve the gods, the temple offered the ultimate opportunity for service. The only purpose for the state — even, in its earliest manifestations, the justification for its survival — was to shelter, maintain, and serve the gods.[1] As the deity's residence, the temple was critical to the ancient Mesopotamians' sense of place in the identity of their cities and the city's own self-identity. Temples were not places where the general populace went to meet personally with the deity, but served as the public face and home of the deity.

Until the 1950s, scholars almost universally characterized the government of the early Mesopotamian city as a "theocracy" and referred to the "temple-city." It was even claimed that at Lagash the temple owned all the land and employed the entire population.[2] In fact, it appears that the temple was not so much the property of the deity but perhaps more the god's "estate," and that it functioned along the lines of a secular institution. Texts record the range of the temple's economic activities as including cultivation of cereals, vegetables, and fruit trees, as well as the control of irrigation waters; management of flocks of sheep and goats, herds of cows and equids; fishing in fresh and salt water; manufacture of textiles, leather, and wooden items, metalwork, and stone; and promotion of trading links with foreign lands. This required storerooms, granaries,

---

1. Wiggermann, "Theologies, Priests, and Worship in Ancient Mesopotamia," 1861.
2. Postgate, *Early Mesopotamia*, 109.

and workshops, for which both archaeological and textual evidence is available.[3]

Archaeologists over the last century and a half have excavated a number of religious structures, yielding physical evidence that reflects the development of religious architecture in Mesopotamia. As with so many other subjects, the Mesopotamians also created lists of temples. These lists are helpful not only for their content, but also for illuminating the underlying principles of organization, which suggest differing emphases among a number of groups at various moments in history.[4]

This chapter will survey general features of the setting and function of the Mesopotamian temples and examine the data available. Since the temple lists may require interpretation as to whether they refer to actual temples and what their ordering may indicate, we will also examine the types of buildings that have been excavated and how those material remains have been interpreted.

General Background

Each Mesopotamian city was home to a deity, and each of the prominent deities was the patron of a city.[5] Mesopotamian culture was urban, so all of the known temples from Mesopotamia were located in cities.[6] Unlike other ancient Near Eastern religions with urban settings, in Mesopotamia there are no references to cultic activity outside the cities, no sanctuaries or cult objects outside cities, nor sacred trees, rocks, rivers, lakes, or seas with cultic significance.[7] Even deities whose origins relate to natural phenom-

---

3. Postgate, *Early Mesopotamia*, 115.

4. George, *House Most High*, 1.

5. Van de Mieroop, *The Ancient Mesopotamian City*, 46.

6. Van De Mieroop, *The Ancient Mesopotamian City*, 215. Note later in this chapter and in Chapter 9 on "Rituals" that references indicate the *akitu* house was located outside the city. However, no rituals were performed there, and it was situated outside the city largely so the deity could then enter the city; Cohen, *The Cultic Calendars of the Ancient Near East*, 404.

7. The only deified rivers were associated with the river ordeal; the river remained nameless in the texts and was associated with the waters of the underworld; van de Mieroop, *The Ancient Mesopotamian City*, 215; Black and Green, *Gods, Demons and Symbols*, 155-56.

ena such as the sun and the planet Venus had cults located in temples within cities.[8] The fortune of the Mesopotamian city was connected to its specific deities, whose divine powers in turn rose and fell with the political status of the deity's city. This is evidenced in the *Enuma Elish,* which reflected the political and cosmic rise of Babylon.

All important temples were located within the walled inner city, with the temple of the oldest patron deity situated in or near the center of town and occupying the highest elevation. There may also have been shrines located in the suburbs.[9] Through numerous rebuildings of the temples, the ground of the oldest tended to be the highest. This may lie behind the concept of the ziggurat, an architectural form developed in the late third millennium. The ziggurat was a tower situated near the temple and connected by courtyards. Though they were built of solid brick and did not house the statue of the deity,[10] their sheer height dominated not only the temple precinct but the city in general.[11]

The temple was literally the "house" of the god and contained the deity's cult image. It was where the god lived with family and servants, ate, drank, slept, was entertained, and worked. In order to thoroughly service the gods, the temple was equipped like a household with essential provisions for the god's meals (kitchens and vessels for making, storing, and serving), sleeping rooms with beds, side rooms for the deity's family, a courtyard with a basin and water for cleansing visitors, and stables for the god's chariot and draft animals.[12]

In their annals and year-dates the Mesopotamian kings report rebuilding dilapidated temples. They also deposited accounts of their activities, as well as the building of the structure and its restoration by their predecessors, in the foundations or walls of buildings, intended only for the eyes of the deity.[13] Since the Mesopotamian kings viewed themselves as the gods' representatives on earth, keeping the deities' homes in order was a primary concern.[14]

8. Van de Mieroop, *The Ancient Mesopotamian City,* 216.

9. Van de Mieroop, *The Ancient Mesopotamian City,* 77.

10. Lloyd, *The Archaeology of Mesopotamia,* 39, 229-30.

11. Lloyd, *The Archaeology of Mesopotamia,* 180-82.

12. Wiggermann, "Theologies, Priests, and Worship," 1861.

13. Ellis, *Foundation Deposits in Ancient Mesopotamia.*

14. Cole and Machinist, *Letters from Priests to the Kings Esarhaddon and Assurbanipal.* These letters reveal the kings' interest in the construction and renovation

Despite numerous excavated examples of temples and ziggurats, no standing buildings remain from before the Parthian period, and no ziggurat remains to its full original height. To some extent this is due to the main building material used: mud. Throughout the ancient Near East mud was used for the walls, floors, pottery, and writing tablets. Mud bricks can be made by hand or shaped in a mold, fired in a kiln, or sun-baked. Mud could be found everywhere and thus was inexpensive, but over thousands of years mud and buildings made from it would decay. As a result, despite the dominance many of these buildings had over the ancient skylines, all of the temples, temple complexes, and ziggurats had to be excavated in order to identify their plans and other details.[15]

Excavated Temples

The present book is not an introduction to Mesopotamian archaeology, so this section will not provide excessive detail about the structures. Still, the developments in the form of the temples, important features common to all of them, and details relevant for specific periods reinforce what we have observed about Mesopotamian religion thus far.

The fundamental features of Mesopotamian temple architecture first appear in the earliest periods under discussion. A series of temples was found at Eridu dating to the Ubaid period (early third millennium). The earliest such place of communal worship, attested in a deep sounding there, was a small, single-room hut, identified through such standard temple features as niched decoration, an "altar," and a mass of blackened fish bones from offerings.[16] Later temples had a standard tripartite division, and the outside façades were buttressed and recessed, in contrast to regular domestic houses, which were stepped in and out.[17]

At Eridu a series of temples was found beneath one corner of a late-Sumerian ziggurat.[18] Actually, this was a temple that continued to be re-

---

of temple edifices in the major cities of the Assyrian Empire, both in the heartland and provinces, even down to minor details of temple and cult.

15. Roaf, "Palaces and Temples in Ancient Mesopotamia," 425.
16. Postgate, *Early Mesopotamia*, 112.
17. Roaf, "Palaces and Temples," 427.
18. Lloyd, *The Archaeology of Mesopotamia*, 39.

built until the first millennium B.C.E. despite the abandonment of the city.[19] Similarly, in the mid-second millennium the Kassites rebuilt the lower temple at Nippur following exactly the plan of the Isin-Larsa temple, which dates three hundred years earlier.[20] What is particularly relevant here is that Eridu, which the Sumerians considered to be the oldest city in the world,[21] reveals some of the oldest religious architecture, and that architecture did not change radically over the course of Mesopotamian history.

In the Uruk period which followed, a series of temples were constructed that introduced features that would become a constant in later ancient Mesopotamian tradition. The Uruk temples were derived from the previous period, but by now the tripartite plan was standardized.[22] Excavators also found an area of courtyards and terraces surrounding a ziggurat dedicated to Inanna and repeatedly rebuilt.[23] One unique feature of the architecture found here and at other sites dating to this period was the use of cone mosaic to decorate the walls.[24]

Typically, the sanctuary chamber of an early Mesopotamian temple was a rectangular space with a door in one of the long sides, at right angles to the wall with the altar ("bent axis approach"). Behind the raised brick altar, a wall-niche marked the position in which the cult statue must have stood. Around the middle of the sanctuary were smaller brick platforms usually named "offering tables" and brick benches along the base of the walls for votive statues. A final feature marking it as a religious building was a buttressed outer façade, with small towers flanking the entrance and a modest annex containing a bread oven. Over time, larger and more elaborate temples developed, adding such elements as a forecourt, which was later surrounded by subsidiary chambers forming a small precinct also entered through an outer gateway with flanking towers.[25]

While the Ur III period is often called a Sumerian revival, a change occurred in the layout of ordinary temples. The "bent-axis" approach was abandoned and replaced with a direct access to the cella, a plan main-

---

19. Roaf, "Palaces and Temples," 427-29.
20. Roaf, "Palaces and Temples," 427-29.
21. Lloyd, *The Archaeology of Mesopotamia*, 39. The Sumerian King List, column i 1.
22. Roaf, "Palaces and Temples," 428.
23. Lloyd, *The Archaeology of Mesopotamia*, 49.
24. Roaf, "Palaces and Temples," 428.
25. Lloyd, *The Archaeology of Mesopotamia*, 120.

Reconstructed façade of the ziggurat at Ur, built by Ur-Namma (21st century B.C.E.) *(K. Smith)*

tained throughout the period covered in this volume. This change meant that the tower-flanked portal and vestibule, ante-cella, and inner sanctuary were now aligned on opposite sides of a central court to create a single vista which ended with the cult statue itself. Components of this schema could be multiplied, but the central features of the plan remained constant.[26]

Religious architecture in general does not change significantly from this point on, with the possible exception of some double temples in Assyria. The Assur temple built by Shamshi-Adad appears to have had two main sanctuaries, with one conforming to the plan adopted in Babylonia during the Ur III period. Much later, in the first millennium, Sennacherib added an eastern annex. Annexed to the Ishtar temple at Assur was a small secondary shrine, where Ishtar was also worshipped, but this one retained the "bent-axis" approach from the third millennium. Two other principal temples in Assyria also had dual dedications and unusual plans: the Anu-Adad shrine had twin ziggurats and an enclosed forecourt, all functioning

26. Lloyd, *The Archaeology of Mesopotamia*, 155.

as part of a single architectural composition, and the Sin and Shamash temple had twin sanctuaries.[27]

The lack of significant change in temple architecture may align with the greater role of personal gods in the second millennium and later centralization of the cult during the periods of Assyrian and Babylonian domination in the first millennium. Interestingly, while temple architecture does not appear to change significantly, which gods are prominent in any particular place or moment does change. Thus, the form of the building apparently accommodates the change in function of the deity who resides there and his or her status.

Another reason for the lack of change over time may correlate to the activity carried out in the temple, especially in the divine sanctuary.[28] Since the Mesopotamian deities were envisioned as having human needs — hence the necessity of humans to do their work — they required regular meals and might even be visited by other gods when they were served something better. Normally the gods were fed twice a day, accompanied by water and beer.[29] On special days more offerings were made, such as the delivery of first-fruits.[30] At other times the deity left the sanctuary to visit other deities or to celebrate special events such as the New Year.[31]

To date the temples found in Mesopotamia comprised not only the sanctuary of the deity but were actually large complexes of buildings, which some scholars would call temple estates.[32] These temple estates were maintained as would be secular institutions and might include property in more than one location. From Girsu, approximately sixteen hundred tablets dating to the mid-third millennium indicate that temple activities required storerooms, granaries, and workshops. Some of these activities could have taken place inside the temple enclosure, but there was not always space.[33] In the Old Babylonian period, the Sin temple at Khafajah stored its grain in different villages, and the temple at Neribtum (Ischali) was engaged in textile production, although no signs of that work have

27. Lloyd, *The Archaeology of Mesopotamia*, 181.
28. Postgate, *Early Mesopotamia*, 117.
29. Postgate, *Early Mesopotamia*, 119-20.
30. Postgate, *Early Mesopotamia*, 123.
31. Postgate, *Early Mesopotamia*, 124.
32. Postgate, *Early Mesopotamia*, 115.
33. Postgate, *Early Mesopotamia*, 115.

been excavated.[34] Thus. these areas technically belonged to the temple but were not necessarily on its premises.

So too, some areas that were part of the temple complexes appear not to be directly related to the cult proceedings. Already in the Early Dynastic period there were houses located in the compounds of major temples.[35] The Ur III–period precinct of Inanna in Nippur included a building so significant as to be a prototype of the later Assyrian palace. The resident of the house was clearly the chief administrator, and his extended family had access to the premises.[36] Though the sanctuary of the deity may have been the main religious focus of the complex, what constituted the temple was more expansive. The point of the temple was not so much a place where people could pray to the deities, but a place where the deity could live and have people take care of him, and so the temple also required the space and resources to produce all that the deity and his retinue needed.

Temple Lists

The ancient Mesopotamians temple lists reveal a variety of organizing principles. Some are organized partly on thematic principles, whereas others appear to be more theologically arranged, grouping temples according to the deity or deities to whom they were dedicated.[37] This section will review the kinds of lists and then briefly discuss the relationship between the lists, the actual temples that have been discovered, and how that impacts our understanding of Mesopotamian religion.

The earliest temple lists recovered are of those that are thematically organized. Andrew George suggests that they came into being when Sumerian compound words or phrases beginning with the element e2, the Sumerian designation for "house," were collected into lists for their own sake, eventually to be incorporated into the great lexical lists. These early lists also include Sumerian temple names.[38]

The most common extant temple lists are geographically arranged. Within this category are lists which focus on a region, and so include sev-

34. Postgate, *Early Mesopotamia,* 115.
35. Zettler, "Administration of the Temple of Inanna at Nippur," 121.
36. Zettler, "Administration of the Temple," 121.
37. George, *House Most High,* 1.
38. George, *House Most High,* 1-2.

eral towns and cities, and others which deal with the sanctuaries of a single location. In these texts, temples are often grouped according to city and may reflect a conscious effort to collect the names of the temples of a particular region, such as Akkad.[39]

Other lists are arranged more theologically, usually grouping the temples according to divine owner. The best example is the Canonical Temple List, which also serves as an important springboard to discussing other issues in the temple lists such as differences between Assyrian and Babylonian lists, dating of texts, and organization.[40] William L. Moran, who coined the modern title, qualified the designation by claiming "by [canonical] we mean only that it was standardized and was in its comprehensiveness *the* temple list."[41] The claim that the text was standardized suggests a process which included other texts and by which this came to be considered by some authoritative body the normative text. The qualification also suggests that the text was regarded important enough to be "the" temple list. One caveat is that this list is known only from copies found in Assurbanipal's libraries in contrast to other temple lists known from many more individual exemplars.[42] Although the list comes from one of the latest and most influential libraries (both in the ancient and modern worlds), it is found only there.

Like other ancient Mesopotamian lexical lists, the Canonical Temple List is arranged with two subcolumns. On the left is each temple's Sumerian ceremonial name, and opposite in the right-hand subcolumn is the explanation "temple of the god So-and-so." Sometimes appended to this name is a geographical comment or, less common, another reference.[43] It is also clear that the majority of sanctuaries listed in the Canonical Temple List were not buildings in their own right but small shrines within larger sacred buildings.[44] The Canonical Temple List then was not as much a directory listing temples as an encyclopedia of ceremonial temple names associated with each deity, underscoring its organization as more theologically driven than geographically structured.[45]

This text highlights a difference of interests among the Assyrian and

39. George, *House Most High*, 41.
40. George, *House Most High*, 4.
41. Quoted by George, *House Most High*, 5.
42. George, *House Most High*, 5.
43. George, *House Most High*, 6.
44. George, *House Most High*, 6.
45. George, *House Most High*, 1.

Babylonian lists. The Canonical Temple List, as preserved, deals mostly with Babylonian cult centers, providing little information about Assyrian temples. This is in contrast to the Assyrian Temple List, known from Nineveh and Assur, which was widely distributed, at least in Sargonid times.[46] That the Canonical Temple List was found in the library of Assurbanipal shows the Assyrian ruler's interest in gathering texts from all over, but also suggests that, even at the height of Assyria's political power, in comparison to Babylonia, Assyria's religious structures were deemed somehow less significant or not considered essential knowledge.

The dating of the Canonical Temple List also addresses changes in the kinds of temple lists and their meaning. Although the Canonical Temple List was found in Assurbanipal's library, some scholars suggest its composition dates to the Kassite period. This earlier dating rests upon the omission of two important sanctuaries of Nabu and another of Belili at Babylon. These are found in the *Tintir* text, which George dates to the reign of Nebuchadnezzar I (1124-1103). That the Canonical List seems unaware of this text, popular and much-copied in both Assyria and Babylonia, suggests that it was composed prior to *Tintir*. Also, since the Canonical Text knows about the reign of the Kassite King Kurigalzu (ca. 1400 B.C.E.) and his new capital of Dur-Kurigalzu, it must date after that time.[47] Thus, even though the Canonical Temple List was composed more than half a century earlier than Assurbanipal and focused primarily on Babylonia, it still garnered the respect or importance to necessitate its presence in the Assyrian monarch's library.

The significance of this text may lie not only in its organization but the order of its entries. The Canonical Temple List appears to be modeled on the Great God List, An=Anum, also compiled in the Kassite period. The order of these lists is, with minimal variation, the same. The beginning of the text is lost, but scholars presume it begins with Anu. The surviving text begins with Enlil and the court of Nippur, including Ninurta, then lists the Mother Goddess and her entourage, followed by Ea and his family, which includes Marduk and Nabu, after which come Sin, Shamash, Adad, and Ishtar and their entourages, and then the junior gods, Gula and the court of Isin, and finally Nergal and other chthonic deities.[48]

The precise relationship of the various places (temples, shrines) incor-

46. George, *House Most High*, 5.
47. George, *House Most High*, 5-6.
48. George, *House Most High*, 6.

porated in the temple lists to those excavated is difficult to ascertain. Because the names in the lists apparently can refer to either a major sanctuary, part of one, or part of a complex makes identifying many of the listed places with known sites difficult. What is clear is that a great amount of care went into building the temples, following a formalized plan for their layout, as well as maintaining an ongoing record of where the various deities, their consorts, and entourages were worshipped. As with much of Mesopotamian literature, the importance of the written lists for groups other than scholars, priests, and kings is not clear. In fact, it is uncertain precisely who was allowed to enter any particular shrine in any specific period. Thus, although for some segment of the ancient Mesopotamian population the temples and their maintenance as well as keeping a written record of where they were and to whom they were dedicated were important, we cannot say how widespread that concern was.

Cult Statues

Mesopotamian temples were the residence of the deities, and the priests made physical manifestations of their deities to live there. All temple rituals were anthropomorphized to serve the cult statue.[49] Much research has been conducted in recent years to understand what and how the ancient Mesopotamians understood the relationship between the anthropomorphized cult statue and the deity the image represented.[50]

These statues were often crafted of a wooden or bitumen core, plated with gold and silver and clothed in costly robes with gold and silver spangles. They could not be too large because the statue had to be portable so it could travel for festivals.[51] Special rituals were conducted to animate the deity.[52] The process by which a cult statue was transformed from a piece of carved stone to the actual manifestation of a deity is through a ritual called the *mīs pî*, or "mouth-washing." By this means, ritual specialists transferred the deity from the spiritual realm to the physical world.[53]

49. Lloyd, *The Archaeology of Mesopotamia*, 1.
50. Winter, "Opening the Eyes and Opening the Mouth."
51. Walker and Dick, *The Induction of the Cult Image in Ancient Mesopotamia*, 6.
52. Walker and Dick, *The Induction of the Cult Image*, 7.
53. Walker and Dick, *The Induction of the Cult Image*, 4, citing Boden, "The Mesopotamian Washing of the Mouth."

The *mīs pî* ritual involved washing the cult statue's mouth. It was also a purificatory rite involving the king or his royal insignia, animals and sacred objects, an ordinary man, and priests. The ritual was primarily a purificatory rite which prepared the object for contact with the divine by washing away impurities. Washing the statue's mouth first appears to have facilitated communication between nondeities and the divine.[54]

On the second day a ritual was performed where the cult statue's mouth was "opened," and only then could the statue enter the temple.[55] This was particularly important, because until its mouth was opened the statue was unable to eat bread, drink water, or smell incense. It thus appears that washing the mouth purified the image from human contamination, but opening the mouth enabled the statue to function as the deity.[56]

Even this important ritual was not enough to consecrate a cult statue. Mesopotamians believed that approval for the presence of the deity in the statue rested with the deity: the deity had to accept the image in order to take it as its own.[57] Once this was done, the statue served as the god in the context of the temple's rituals. The connection between the deity and its cult statue explains why, when temples were destroyed and the image was carried off, usually in times of war, the people viewed it as the deity abandoning them and the city.[58]

Akītu House

The *akītu* house is discussed here because it is a templelike structure, though rather different from those shrines discussed thus far. Unlike all of those temples, this structure was outside the city walls.[59] In third-millennium Ur it was located at a nearby site, but according to a Middle Assyrian ritual text from Assur it had to be reached by barge.[60] The details of the festival in which the *akītu* house played a role will be discussed in Chapter 9 on "Rituals."

54. Walker and Dick, *The Induction of the Cult Image,* 10-12.
55. Walker and Dick, *The Induction of the Cult Image,* 16.
56. Walker and Dick, *The Induction of the Cult Image,* 14.
57. Walker and Dick, *The Induction of the Cult Image,* 8.
58. Oppenheim, *Ancient Mesopotamia,* 184.
59. Cohen, *The Cultic Calendars,* 403.
60. Cohen, *The Cultic Calendars,* 418.

In further contrast with the other temples, nothing of great significance appears to have happened at the *akītu* house. The deities were fed there, but few of the important events in the *Akītu* festival occurred at that site. For example, in Babylon the reading of the *Enuma Elish* to Marduk and the humbling of the king took place in Babylon, and neither in Babylon nor Uruk did the determining of destiny by the gods take place at the *akītu* house.[61]

Apparently its main function was as a temporary residence for the chief god of the city until it was time for that deity to reenter the city.[62] The deity could not do so with all the requisite pomp and circumstance if it were still within the city. Thus, though the *akītu* house serves as a temple of sorts for the deity outside the city, its real role is to provide the deity a means of entering the city.

Conclusions

The ancient Mesopotamian temples were complex, highly-organized, heavily-staffed organizations. Their origin dates to the earliest period when we can discuss religion in Mesopotamia, and many of their fundamental features did not change radically through time. The concept of a temple, because of the significance of the building and what it housed, was so important as to be addressed in the important ancient Mesopotamian science of lists. The *akītu* house, while a temple of sorts, reinforced the glory and importance of the deities by providing a place outside the city so that they could enter it again, triumphantly. The temples housed the gods and all that they needed. How the temples were staffed, what the personnel performed, and how they earned their roles is therefore the next step in understanding Mesopotamian religion.

61. Cohen, *The Cultic Calendars*, 403-4.
62. Cohen, *The Cultic Calendars*, 404.

CHAPTER 7

Religious Personnel

M any types of religious personnel served in ancient Mesopotamian society, including priests (male and female), cult personnel, diviners, and "magicians." Since the line between religion and other spheres was not distinct, even kings constituted a class of religious functionary, but because their situation is more complicated, and some Mesopotamian kings were actually deified, they will be treated in a separate chapter. Many of the functions performed by religious personnel were not segregated to the divine realm but incorporated everything from the king's rule to medicine.

Again, we will provide a general survey of the kinds of religious personnel and then trace a few to show how particular offices evolved over time or place, to reveal both the stream of tradition and change. Specifically, we will examine priests, temple officers, diviners, magicians, and a special category of women devotes called *nadītu*.

Maintaining the Temples

There is no native Mesopotamian word for "priest." All who served or serviced the gods in the temple setting were religious personnel. This included chief attendants, lamentation priests who chanted in the temples, musicians to sing songs properly, as well as individuals to sweep the floors.[1] The office that most think of as "high priest" goes back to the earli-

---

1. See the list in Postgate, *Early Mesopotamia*, 127.

est periods in Mesopotamia and, as suggested in Chapter 5 on "The Gods," especially in regard to Inanna/Ishtar there was barely a line between the religious and political.

The origins of the priesthood in Mesopotamia appear to be rooted in what is regarded as the third stage of societal changes connected to urban civilization. In this stage, following the development of agriculture and specialization as a result of stable surplus in food production that created different classes, the upper strata in the social hierarchy gained control of the administration of society. In Mesopotamia, the first group to take charge was the priesthood. The main function of the temples in the early period was one of economic distribution based on large and complex temple estates, as seen in the previous chapter.[2] The priests justified their leadership on religious grounds.[3] The important role of priests and the religious hierarchy is already firmly established in the Jemdet Nasr period (ca. 2900 B.C.E.), as evidenced by a hierarchical list containing a record of professions. This list begins with the highest officials, followed by other officials and then priests. Among the group of highest officials, two, the *en* and the *sanga*, were the highest-ranking officers of the temple household.[4]

Over time, particularly as the cities began fighting with each other, the role of the priesthood changed. The king fought battles against other city-states, couched in the language of protecting the property of the city-god. The Umma and Lagash conflict, which dates to the twenty-fourth century, is a paradigm for this transition. The conflict lasted more than a century and is pitched as a defense of the rights of the god Ningirsu with Eanatum, one of the kings of Lagash, even portraying himself as having been bred as Ningirsu's champion, nurtured by Ninhursag.[5]

The priests' roots were thus administrative, both in organizing the city and the temple complexes. Another list enumerates temple personnel from various temples. The staff at Ninurta's temple at Lagash included the high priest, lamentation priest, purification priest, high priestess, *nadītu* priestess, chief *qadishtum* priestess, diviner, snake-charmer, miller, guard, fuller, fuel-

2. Van de Mieroop, *The Ancient Mesopotamian City,* 27.
3. Van de Mieroop, *The Ancient Mesopotamian City,* 27.
4. Robertson, "The Social and Economic Organization of Ancient Mesopotamian Temples," 449.
5. Van de Mieroop, *The Ancient Mesopotamian City,* 33. Translation of the text for this can be found in Magid, "Sumerian Early Dynastic Royal Inscriptions," 11-15.

Statue of a priest from the Square Temple of Abu, Tell Asmar, Iraq (early third millennium). *(Courtesy of the Oriental Institute, University of Chicago)*

carrier, water-carrier, oil-presser, cow-herder, (copper-) smith, steward, boatman, boat-tower, weaver, courtyard-sweeper, barber, water-purer, mat-maker, runner, stone-carver, king's butler, palace guard, house supervisor, accountant, treasurer, cupbearer, overseer of the oilpresses, and scribe.[6] Since most of the Mesopotamian lists are hierarchically ordered, this seems to be the case here as well. From this list of temple personnel, it is clear that a large range of people were necessary for the proper running of the temples.

The range of necessary personnel is not surprising in light of the tasks they performed in the temples. Among their responsibilities were caring

6. Postgate, *Early Mesopotamia*, 127.

for the gods' needs, placing offerings before them, keeping them clothed and sheltered, and performing rituals. [7] In the third millennium, priestesses functioned as the chief attendants to male deities and priests served female deities.[8]

While the high priests served some of the more important cultic roles for the temple, the majority of the personnel, as is evident from the list, performed more mundane tasks. Because the temples could be regarded as estates, those who worked the fields and swept the floors were technically religious personnel insofar as their primary job was to care for the deities.

A number of texts offer insight into how specific temple administrators functioned, at least at one temple in one city in one period. Texts from Ur, dating to the Ur III period, indicate that the chief administrator was the "public face" of the temple of Inanna and was responsible for the receipt of commodities into the temple, but also had cultic and judicial responsibilities. This position was heritable and passed from father to son through four generations during this period.[9]

The texts from the house of Ur-me-me reveal that a number of the extended kin group connected to the chief administrators was also tied to the temple.[10] Detailed analysis of the texts reveals that family members were involved in financial matters dealing with temple property although they had no official capacity at the time of the transaction.[11] Thus it is not surprising that in this archive a son brings charges against his father, including:

> infringing a cultic taboo, . . . intercepting (and diverting) the sheep, the butter, and flour for the royal offering, . . . intercepting the butter for the regular offerings amounting to three sila per month, and . . . diluting the butter of the regular offering.

These charges were brought before a high-ranking panel which included the governor of Nippur (and a relative of the father and son) and the *sanga*

7. Nemet-Nejat, *Daily Life in Ancient Mesopotamia,* 191.

8. Note in Chapter 5 on "The Gods" that Enheduanna was technically the high priestess of the moon-god Nanna, even though she wrote extensively of how Inanna helped her maintain or possibly even recover that position.

9. Zettler, "Administration of the Temple," 125.

10. Zettler, "Administration of the Temple," 125.

11. Zettler, "Administration of the Temple," 128.

of Enlil. The son could not substantiate the charges and thus was condemned to death.[12]

These samples from one temple archive reveal both the responsibilities of the chief administrator and how a system can be corrupted. The specific example here dates to the third millennium, but texts from the Neo-Assyrian period also attest to shepherds in charge of flocks of sheep destined for sacrifice in Assur who refused to bring in the animals, a cook who stole a golden statue of the plague-god Erra, drunken prefects ensconced outside the gates of Assur who stole the exit tolls they collected, a priest of Ea who stole gold from a temple offering table, and a ring of clerical criminals who cut off and removed gold appendages from the cella of the god to whom they were supposedly devoted.[13]

Corruption of the system is not difficult to imagine considering that the expense of such an elaborate temple system was fairly large. Religious personnel received food, drinks, textiles, wool, and silver goods. As with other spheres of religion in Mesopotamia, beginning in the Old Babylonian period the regular staff was reduced. Gaining a job in a temple depended on the type of service, the period of time, and connections. As noted earlier regarding the goddess Inanna/Ishtar, beginning with Sargon the office of high priestess for the moon-god Nanna became an appointed position by the most powerful king in Mesopotamia. Other offices required specialists, such as craftsmen, scribes, and other permanent administrators.[14] In other periods, as in the example above, many of these offices became inherited positions.

Diviners

Since humans existed to serve the gods, the responsibility of the diviner was to learn what the gods wanted. The ancient Mesopotamians believed the gods disclosed their intentions by signs in natural phenomena and world events that needed to be interpreted through prolonged observation and study. This was accomplished by means of omens, a practice which be-

12. Zettler, "Administration of the Temple," 128-29.

13. Cole and Machinist, *Letters from Priests to the Kings Esarhaddon and Assurbanipal,* xviii.

14. Nemet-Nejat, *Daily Life in Ancient Mesopotamia,* 192.

came a science in Mesopotamia as evidenced in many omen treatises.[15] Omens could be solicited or unsolicited.[16] Diviners were specialists who solicited omens from the gods and interpreted the signs.[17] They could communicate with the divine by various means: extispicy (animal entrails), hepatoscopy (liver), leconomancy (throwing stones into water), and libanomancy (incense smoke). All branches of Babylonian divination are based on the fundamental idea that events in the universe are related to one another: if one of these would occur, its correlate might be expected. By communicating with the gods through divination, humans could learn about the deities' decisions and possibly influence them.[18]

Extispicy is one of the better known modes of divination in Mesopotamia because of the large number of tablets devoted to the subject. While examining the liver of an animal to determine the future or what the deities want from humans appears in the modern world to be a trivial superstition, in Babylonia it was an intellectual effort sustained over many centuries. The practice was based on the idea that entrails, primarily the liver, of a sacrificial sheep mirror future events pertaining to each of its features.[19]

As with other areas, there are stages of development in Mesopotamian extispicy. No evidence points to the Sumerians practicing anything this extensive, other than seeking yes or no answers as to whether a candidate for cultic office was acceptable to the god or whether the deity permitted his temple to be rebuilt.[20] Only in the late Old Babylonian period did extispicy become a recognized source of knowledge, and it is then that the first compendia were written. All of the Old Babylonian compendia take the form of contemporary letters, with nothing suggesting that the scribes were specialists or that the contents were secret.[21] The process of serialization of the individual chapters began in the Old Babylonian period, evident from five different types of compendia that survive.[22] The next stage in the development of written series is not clear, but the material was gradually

15. For a wonderful introduction to the whole field of extispicy in Babylonia, see Koch-Westenholz, *Babylonian Liver Omens*.

16. Oppenheim, *Ancient Mesopotamia*, 206-27.

17. Note their importance to the ruling kings; Starr, *Queries to the Sungod*.

18. Koch-Westenholz, *Babylonian Liver Omens*, 12-13.

19. Koch-Westenholz, *Babylonian Liver Omens*, 7, 13.

20. Koch-Westenholz, *Babylonian Liver Omens*, 13.

21. Koch-Westenholz, *Babylonian Liver Omens*, 14-15.

22. Koch-Westenholz, *Babylonian Liver Omens*, 17.

standardized, with some components of earlier texts being dropped from the corpus. It is not clear precisely when the omen series attained textual stability and a fixed sequence of tablets, thus becoming "canonical," but most scholars suggest this took place sometime during the last centuries of the second millennium.[23] What is remarkable about the final canon of the omen series is that the various Neo-Assyrian manuscripts from Nimrud and Nineveh and the contemporary Babylonian manuscripts duplicate almost exactly, meaning the series was closed from 750 B.C.E. to Seleucid times, with no evidence for locally-variant "recensions." This suggests that not only were the texts important but it was also significant that they be precise, not surprising in light of the way in which they were used. Thus the people who conducted extispicy and those scribes who copied the texts were specialists who took their roles quite seriously.

Other outlets were available for trying to understand the future and to manipulate it. The goal of the magician and sorcerer was to influence humans' success on earth. Also, numerous incantations were performed by a range of personnel.[24] The incantation series *Shurpu* was a collection of spells and rituals for all types of misbehavior: cultic negligence, domestic trouble, uncharitable conduct, cruelty to animals, and unintentional contact with ritually unclean people or places.[25] Astronomy in Mesopotamia associated signs in the sky with terrestrial events, usually concerning the king or the country.[26]

The majority of religious personnel were connected to the state cult and part of a hierarchical organization. Many of them were specialists who were trained in one aspect of divination. They needed to know and consult specific texts, so special training was clearly required. Since the Mesopotamians believed that people were to serve the gods, knowing what the deities wanted was serious business.

Prophecy

Another category of discerning what the deities wanted or demanded has only recently come to light. Prophetic texts have been discovered that pro-

---

23. Koch-Westenholz, *Babylonian Liver Omens,* 20-21, 26.
24. Foster, *Before the Muses,* 1:113-45; 2:840-98.
25. Nemet-Nejat, *Daily Life in Ancient Mesopotamia,* 197.
26. Rochberg, "Astronomy and Calendars in Ancient Mesopotamia."

vide new information about an area of Assyrian and Babylonian religion previously unknown. The study of prophecy is complicated because it was originally thought to have been native to Israel, so the appearance of prophets outside the biblical text has demanded biblicists to rethink the originality of prophecy in Israelite religion.[27] These prophetic texts reveal the existence of "inspired" prophecy in the ancient Near East, particularly at Mari and Assyria. In the Assyrian context, the prophecies are closely linked to the cult of Ishtar and to Assyrian royal ideology, mythology, and iconography.[28]

"Prophecy" can be defined as "the transmission of allegedly divine messages by a human intermediary to a third party."[29] The prophets of the biblical text, many of whom have books named after them and/or their mission, tend to overshadow our understanding of what prophecy was, how it was conducted, and who was a prophet, even though these ideas do not necessarily apply to ancient Mesopotamian prophets. In the ancient Near East in general there are some commonalities. All prophets deliver communications from the divine world, normally for a third party, and serve as mediators who may or may not identify with the deity; they draw upon inspiration through ecstasy, dreams, or "inner illumination.[30] Two ancient Mesopotamian sites produced texts suggesting that prophets received messages from the deities: Mari and Assyria.

The Mari texts date to the eighteenth century B.C.E., specifically the reign of Zimri-Lim, and contain numerous accounts of people speaking or hearing oracles, usually while they are in shrines. Information about the prophet, if it exists, is usually embedded in a letter referring to the situation, but in general the individual identity of the prophet was of little concern to his or her contemporaries.[31] Prophets are identified by a number of different titles, including *apilum/apiltum* ("answerer"), *muhhum/muhutum* ("ecstatic"), *assinnum* ("cult singer"), and *nabu* ("one called").[32] The titles are provided by the correspondents and reflect how the commu-

27. Now that all the extant Mesopotamian prophetic texts have been published, there is a great interest in it in the Society of Biblical Literature. See, e.g., Nissinen, *Prophecy in Its Ancient Near Eastern Context*.

28. Parpola, *Assyrian Prophecies*, xv.

29. Nissinen, "Preface," in *Prophecy in Its Ancient Near Eastern Context*, vii.

30. Huffmon, "A Company of Prophets," 48.

31. Van der Toorn, "Mesopotamian Prophecy between Immanence and Transcendence," 78.

32. Huffmon, "A Company of Prophets," 49.

nity views the prophet; they are not forms of self-identification. Prophets are both male and female. The prophets' inspiration is not always indicated, but usually they receive their messages in a dream, in a temple, by going to a temple in a dream, or through some form of extispicy.[33]

Though the messages are taken seriously by the political authorities, this is not the preferred means of communication with the deities. In order for any prophet's oracle to be considered authentic, the prophets submit with the report some of their hair and mantle fringe so the revelations could be confirmed through divination. The Mari prophetic reports were subject to review, sometimes by Queen Shiptu through special divination and other times through extispicy.[34]

The messages are virtually all addressed to the king, though this may not reflect the nature of prophetic concern but the fact that the texts were recovered from a royal archive.[35] The messages usually assure the king of success or warn of possible danger. Some messages express concern about specific cultic acts, such as special sacrifices that have been neglected, though these too are usually projected as in the best interests of the king.[36] Within the corpus a large number of deities are mentioned: Addu, Addu of Halab, Addu of Kallassu, Dagan, Dagan of Tuttul, Dagan of Subatum, Marduk, Nergal, and Shamash. The prophets as well are connected with a similarly large number of deities.[37]

The situation in Assyria was slightly different. These prophetic texts date from the Neo-Assyrian period and are written in literary Neo-Assyrian, which is not that common for the period.[38] Unlike Mari, the majority of the Assyrian prophecies are preserved as part of a collection of tablets, not as the original record of the incident in letters.[39] Because of this format of preservation, the prophet's location during most of the prophecy's occurrence is not clear, though it was clearly less connected to a temple than was the case at Mari.[40] Also, none of the titles known from

33. Huffmon, "A Company of Prophets," 56.

34. Huffmon, "A Company of Prophets," 50.

35. A few focus on local people and what they should do; Huffmon, "A Company of Prophets," 53.

36. Huffmon, "A Company of Prophets," 53-54.

37. Huffmon, "A Company of Prophets," 49.

38. Huffmon, "A Company of Prophets," 57.

39. Huffmon, "A Company of Prophets," 59.

40. Van der Toorn, "Mesopotamian Prophecy," 83.

Mari occurs in these oracle texts. Instead, the Assyrian texts use the specifically Neo-Assyrian term *raggimu/raggintu* ("proclaimer"), though some are ascribed to a *seletu* ("votaress").[41] The prophetic reports identify the speakers by name and place of residence.[42] The Assyrian texts list fewer deities. In fact, the overwhelming majority of Neo-Assyrian prophets are connected somehow with the cult of Ishtar. When deities other than Ishtar address the king through prophecy, they use the channel of a prophet of Ishtar.[43]

As at Mari, the extant letters indicate that the prophets were involved in matters affecting the kingship.[44] Possibly because of the nature of the mesages, as also the case at Mari, Esarhaddon and Assurbanipal, the relevant Assyrian kings, took the prophets seriously. In fact, the Assyrians may have taken prophecy even more seriously because there is little evidence for a process of verification except for dangerous or unfavorable prophecies.[45]

Prophetic activity in ancient Mesopotamia was initiated by the deities coming to the prophets, and both the Old Babylonian Mari documents and those from Assyria suggest a fair amount of scrutiny of what the prophets said. In Mari the prophecies had to be verified by specialists. In Assyria, the fact that the prophecies were collected and listed shows that these prophecies were carefully studied and were examined by specialists. So, while prophecy was less regulated than the activities of some other types of religious personnel, even this showed organization.

Nadītu

While the majority of religious personnel have administrative responsibilities and/or are in direct contact with the deities, another group of individuals expressed devotion or connection to gods by what today we might categorize as personal piety. A class of women referred to as *nadītu* were dedicated to one particular deity and spent a great deal of time praying to

---

41. Huffmon, "A Company of Prophets," 57.
42. Huffmon, "A Company of Prophets," 58.
43. Van der Toorn, "Mesopotamian Prophecy," 78.
44. Huffmon, "A Company of Prophets," 60.
45. Huffmon, "A Company of Prophets," 61.

that deity. The term *nadītum* means "fallow" and appears to refer to the fact that these women were unmarried and not allowed to have children.[46]

At the site of Sippar in southern Mesopotamia an Old Babylonian "cloister" was excavated in the vicinity of the main temple of the city-god Shamash. This consisted of a large walled enclosure, separate from though close to the main temple, containing houses, streets, and even a garden plot. Apparently the area was the residence of a whole community of *nadītu*, some of high birth, including a daughter of Zimri-Lim, king of Mari.[47] Rather than marrying, the woman was entitled to a dowry to set her up in a new home and, according to the Code of Hammurabi, she was permitted a life interest in property given to her by her father.[48]

While Sippar may be the best known archaeologically, other *nadītu* communities were located at Nippur and Babylon. Many of the documents referring to the *nadītu* concern business and family relationships, suggesting that even at Sippar they were not completely reclusive. In fact, at Nippur there is no evidence that they lived in a separate cloister, although they were celibate.[49]

What we know about the *nadītu* women is primarily from one period, and mostly one site, and thus may be a phenomenon that is peculiar to a time and place. Most of the references to the *nadītum* date to the period between the fall of Ur III and the rise of Hammurabi. In the Ur III period, women somewhat equivalent to *nadītum* were attached to the royal court, functioning as a type of subsidiary spouse of the king.[50] These women had dowries for the length of their lives, but apparently because they did not have children, upon their deaths the dowry would revert back to the family, especially their brothers. Some scholars suggest that this was one means of keeping property within the family in a period when women could inherit. It is difficult today to determine whether the *nadītu* women were solely a group dedicated to the worship of a deity or represented an economic arrangement designed by brothers to keep property within the family, or perhaps some combination thereof.

46. *CAD* N I, 63; Stone, "The Social Role of the Naditu Woman in Old Babylonian Nippur."

47. Postgate, *Early Mesopotamia*, 130-31.

48. Laws of Hammurabi §§178-80.

49. Postgate, *Early Mesopotamia*, 131.

50. Postgate, *Early Mesopotamia*, 131.

Conclusions

What falls under the classification of religious personnel in this treatment is rather vast but reflective of the ancient Mesopotamian approach to religion. If people are on earth to serve the deities, then it makes sense that people working in the temples, the religious personnel, would be devoted to that service. It is also not surprising that a category of personnel would be focused on determining precisely what it is that the gods wanted or demanded.

CHAPTER 8

Religious Texts

The definition of "religion" in this volume is rather broad, so quite a range of textual material could be considered "religious." According to A. Leo Oppenheim, only three types of cuneiform (and some other text groups and passages) are important for an understanding of religion: prayers, mythological texts, and ritual texts.[1] Mythological texts will not be considered here because, as noted in Chapter 4, it is not clear that the texts are more religious than literary. Instead, other groups not treated by Oppenheim as "religious" will be reviewed, including disputations, lists, ritual texts, prayers, hymns, some wisdom literature, and historical inscriptions. Note that none of these categories is clearly defined or distinct from some other genres, and many of these genres are associated with rituals that will be addressed in the next chapter.

The wider range of texts to be addressed stems from the idea that religion was not a peripheral category that could be separated from the Mesopotamian worldview.[2] Categorizing texts is always fraught with problems, and some may disagree with my choices here. The point of including these texts is to highlight how infused religion was in the Mesopotamian worldview, introduce a wide range of textual types to show how many different areas contribute to understanding Mesopotamian religion, and to

---

1. Oppenheim, *Ancient Mesopotamia*, 175.

2. Some of these ideas are treated by Oppenheim, but in his chapter on Mesopotamian Psychology rather than under the guise of "religion"; *Ancient Mesopotamia*, 198-206.

provide examples of the different approaches the Mesopotamians took to the same or a similar topic.

Disputations

The disputations, if treated as religious, are often approached as mythological texts, because many scholars consider them a primary source for discussing the ancient Mesopotamian idea of cosmogony, or the origins of the world.[3] However, these texts have their own unique format and style. Also, as a discussion between sometimes inanimate objects, disputations could be considered philosophical in a way usually not attributed to mythological texts.

This is a widely attested genre, particularly popular in the Old Babylonian scribal schools and, according to the texts themselves, at the royal court.[4] In them, two beings, animate or inanimate, debate which is more noble and useful, each emphasizing its own special traits.[5] Many of the accounts tend to be heavy with satire, clever, and humorous.[6] Most disputations begin with a cosmogony, so labeled because it mentions the place of the debaters in the origin of the universe. At the end of the debate, the winner is declared, often by a deity.[7]

The texts usually begin with a statement such as "When upon the Hill of Heaven and Earth, An had spawned the divine Godlings, — Since godly Wheat had not been spawned or created with them, Nor had the yarn of the godly Weaver been fashioned in the Land,"[8] or "[In long-gone, far-off days], after the kind fate had been decreed, [After An and Enlil] had set up the rules of heaven and earth."[9] The cosmogonic introductions are long, taking up to a third of compositions such as Ewe and Grain, and Summer and Winter.[10] The problem with these texts as good cosmogonies is that, to a large extent,

3. In particular, see Clifford, *Creation Accounts in the Ancient Near East and in the Bible*.

4. Vanstiphout, "Disputations," in *COS*, 1:575.

5. Clifford, *Creation Accounts*, 25.

6. Vanstiphout, "Disputations," in *COS*, 1:578.

7. Clifford, *Creation Accounts*, 25.

8. Vanstiphout, "The Disputation Between Ewe and Wheat," in *COS*, 1:575.

9. Vanstiphout, "The Disputation Between Bird and Fish," *COS*, 1:581.

10. Clifford, *Creation Accounts*, 27.

Building inscription of Assurbanipal from Nemet-Enlil, the inner wall of Babylon's double city walls. *(Pergamon Museum, Berlin; photo by Allen Myers)*

they do not deal with how the world was created, but rather how and why the gods created specific things within the world. Thus, they actually serve more like texts such as *Enuma Elish,* which address why people were created rather than how or why the world itself was formed.

While these texts may not shed a great deal of light on why or how the ancient Mesopotamians thought the world was created, they do address other features of the world that could be considered as having some religious or philosophical significance in terms of shaping the ancient Mesopotamian worldview. For example, the characters in the cosmogonic section of the disputations function as prototypes, and the disputation links the disputants to their origin, the time when their destiny was determined.[11] Thus, the disputations reveal that, on some levels, all components of the world were created by the gods for a particular purpose.

The Disputation Between the Hoe and Plow addresses the case of the

11. Clifford, *Creation Accounts,* 27.

common man against the rich and mighty.[12] The Disputation Between Bird and Fish focuses on the importance of pleasant and beautiful things in life over dour sentiments.[13] One's definition of religion will determine whether or not these topics constitute religious or philosophical issues. Furthermore, because the beginning of the Disputation Between the Hoe and Plow does not include a cosmological statement, or any other overt reference to a deity, this may keep some from treating it as a "religious" document. In any case, the disputations are unique, quite fun to read, and yet another forum for the ancient Mesopotamians to ask fundamental questions about their world.

Lists

Lists have already been mentioned, because lists are extant for specific topics including gods, temples, temple personnel, and professions. Only a few observations need be included here that address what this genre says about the ancient Mesopotamians' view of the world and how it was organized.

According to Oppenheim, the lists were originally intended for teaching purposes but eventually became the only accepted method of scholarly presentation.[14] Regardless of the reason for their origin and whether or not there were other forms of legitimate scholarly presentation, it is clear that these lists hold a high position in Mesopotamia scholarship because of both the vast number recovered and the wide range of topics addressed in them.

While the extant lists cover many subjects, for purposes of understanding ancient Mesopotamian religion those that were topically arranged are most relevant. These are attested at a very early period and become increasingly important.[15] Lists of nouns are organized in large groupings. Originally they were sequences of Sumerian nouns with the classifying element in initial position serving as a criterion for the arrangement of the entries. Later they were provided with Akkadian translations. These cover topics such as names of trees, wooden objects, stars,

---

12. Vanstiphout, "The Disputation Between Hoe and Plow," in *COS*, 1:578.
13. Vanstiphout, "The Disputation Between Bird and Fish," in *COS*, 1:581.
14. Oppenheim, *Ancient Mesopotamia*, 244.
15. Oppenheim, *Ancient Mesopotamia*, 246.

and garments. Eventually some of the Akkadian words became obsolete, so a new series was added containing a second Akkadian column with explanation.[16] The question raised by these lists is determination of their organizing principle — whether they show how the ancient Mesopotamians ordered their universe or, as Oppenheim stressed, whether they are operational.[17]

It is quite possible that in some cases these lists can be both. As is clear from the professions list and the god list, those placed on the top of the list clearly were considered more "important." Thus, the rest of the list appears to be organizing them from more important to less important. Simply because the name of a deity or profession appears on a list indicates that it exists and thus has some worth and/or merit. It does not seem difficult then to assert that these lists reflect some organizational principles behind the world.

Also, what may have started as a teaching tool turned into a major science within ancient Mesopotamia, which suggests some preference, at least by the scribal schools and/or scribes, for organizing material in this way. For example, a list named *ana ittishu* contains legal formulas to train scribes for the correct phrasing of deeds and contracts.[18] Thus, the fact that all things, even legal concepts, could be presented in these lists is insight into ancient Mesopotamians' organization of the universe. Note none of these texts provide explanations for the organizational scheme.

Ritual Texts

Ritual texts describe the specific rites to be performed by priests and priestly technicians in the sanctuary. These detailed texts provide the individual acts of a ritual, the prayers and formulae to be recited, and the offerings and sacrificial apparatus required.[19] As noted above in the discussion about the temples and statues of the deities, certain rituals had to be conducted daily, such as feeding the gods. Others were on a yearly cycle, such as the New Year festival, and still others, such as opening the mouth of a

---

16. Oppenheim, *Ancient Mesopotamia*, 247.
17. Oppenheim, *Ancient Mesopotamia*, 248.
18. Oppenheim, *Ancient Mesopotamia*, 248.
19. Oppenheim, *Ancient Mesopotamia*, 178.

statue, were performed as needed. As in other areas, these texts tell us what the ancient Mesopotamians did, or were supposed to do, but not what or how they felt about it.

The available texts suggest that there was a ritual or prayer for almost any concern. Many are intended to ward off something from happening or as a direct result of something having happened. Benjamin Foster has an entire section devoted to what he labels "Devotional and Ritual Poetry," in which he translates a broad range of rituals and prayers, intended, for example, to avert thunder[20] and lightning,[21] against pestilence[22] and snakes, as well as lustration rituals. Most of the texts are hymns which are part of the rites. The very range of topics for which there are texts to be read during a ritual suggests the wide range of observances, the details of which will be discussed in the next chapter.

Prayers

Since technically a prayer is "an earnest request; entreaty; supplication,"[23] it is not surprising that rituals would include prayers since in the religious situation in ancient Mesopotamia these set rites are intended to influence the deities. Oppenheim cites prayers as his first category of texts important for understanding Mesopotamian religion and highlights their link to rituals.[24]

According to Oppenheim, the rituals are carefully described in a section at the end of the prayer which addresses either the praying person or the religious personnel officiating. Like the ritual acts, the prayers are of fixed form, with little variation and few departures from existing patterns, including a limited number of invocations, demands, complaints, and expressions of thanksgiving.[25] Despite this limited range, it is not surprising that extant prayers exist for many of the deities and express desires for numerous gifts.[26]

20. Foster, *Before the Muses*, 2:545.
21. Foster, *Before the Muses*, 2:547.
22. Foster, *Before the Muses*, 2:575.
23. *Webster's New World Dictionary: Second Collegiate Edition*, 1119.
24. Oppenheim, *Ancient Mesopotamia*, 175.
25. Oppenheim, *Ancient Mesopotamia*, 175.
26. For the range of deities to whom prayers are offered and for what, see Foster, *Before the Muses*, 2:491-690.

Hymns

Hymns are somewhat similar to prayers in that they offer praise for the deity, but hymns do not appear to ask the deity for anything.[27] The term "Hymn" comes from the Greek, and from the time of Homer on means a song of praise in honor of the gods, heroes, and conquerors, an appropriate definition for many texts we find under this category. As in worship today, there were times when the ancient Mesopotamians simply praised their deities. Foster avoids the difficulty in differentiating between hymns and prayers in his section "Great Hymns and Prayers," eliminating the problem of ascertaining a request behind the praise.[28]

The range of hymns is fairly extensive, with hymns offered to numerous deities for different topics. The praise in these texts often reinforces our general notions gleaned about various deities from other sources. For example, Ea, the god of wisdom and skill, of which magic is one aspect, was a favorite among diviners and exorcists.[29] Many common deities are the focus of hymns, including Marduk,[30] Ishtar,[31] and Shamash.[32] These texts reveal humans praising their deities for bringing rain, illuminating the darkness (both actual and metaphorical), and prosperity.

Wisdom Literature

An understanding of Wisdom literature is complicated, because the term "wisdom" with regard to a literary genre was originally coined for use with biblical material; therefore, as applied to any other body of material it will be something of a misnomer.[33] As W. G. Lambert observes, the Akkadian term for wisdom is *nēmequ*, and there are several adjectives for "wise," but rarely are they used with moral content. Instead, in Akkadian "wisdom" refers to skill in cult and magic lore, where the wise man is the

27. *Webster's New World Dictionary,* 689.
28. Foster, *Before the Muses,* 2:ix.
29. Benjamin R. Foster, *From Distant Days: Myths, Tales, and Poetry of Ancient Mesopotamia* (Bethesda: CDL, 1995), 223.
30. Foster, *From Distant Days,* 224-26, 247-48.
31. Foster, *From Distant Days,* 238-46.
32. Foster, *From Distant Days,* 224-26, 254-66.
33. Murphy, "Wisdom in the OT."

initiate.[34] Since in this volume there is no association demanded between morality and the cult of the deities, and the cult of the deities most certainly was one of the primary foci of ancient Mesopotamian religion, an initiate in that cult is definitely within the range of relevance.

The wisdom literature of ancient Mesopotamia deals with ethics, practical advice on living, and intellectual problems inherent in the then current outlook on life and includes fables, popular sayings, and proverbs.[35] In terms of our focus on religion, what is found in many of these texts is a questioning of the gods for what has happened to various individuals, an effort to understand humans' role in the universe, the role of personal piety, and why human existence apparently demands suffering.

The Poem of the Righteous Sufferer *(Ludlul bēl nēmeqi)* is possibly the best example of ancient Mesopotamian wisdom literature addressing the concerns of religion, as it existed and was defined by the ancients.[36] In this tablet (the beginning is not preserved) the narrator is forsaken by his gods. This leads to his being shunned, which is apparently what truly upsets him. According to the text,

> the King, the flesh of the gods, the sun of his peoples, his heart is enraged (with me), . . . the courtiers plot hostile action against me, they assemble themselves and give utterance to impious words . . . they combine against me in slander and lies. . . . I, who strode along as a noble, have learned to slip by unnoticed. Though a dignitary, I have become a slave.[37]

Things then turn even worse because all sorts of diseases afflict him, yet nothing the diviner does helps, which leads him to contemplate the purpose for the suffering of the righteous.[38] Finally, his deliverance is promised in three dreams, leading to his freedom from disease.[39] In the last dream, a messenger who is called an incantation priest appears carrying a tablet. He announces that he is a messenger of Marduk and has brought

---

34. Lambert, *Babylonian Wisdom Literature,* 1.
35. Lambert, *Babylonian Wisdom Literature,* 1.
36. Lambert, *Babylonian Wisdom Literature,* 21-62.
37. Lambert, *Babylonian Wisdom Literature,* 33-35.
38. Lambert, *Babylonian Wisdom Literature,* 41.
39. Lambert, *Babylonian Wisdom Literature,* 41-46.

the man (who is finally named Shubshi-meshre-Shakkan) prosperity.[40] The text does not explain whether the man did anything specific to turn Marduk's favor, nor is the definition of piety explained. Though the text has a happy ending, the capriciousness of the deities, and thus the man's uncertain future, is not dissipated.

Historical Inscriptions

Historical texts in general are not considered religious documents, but the ancient Mesopotamian kings were loath to exclude the deities when referencing their deeds, and there are numerous references to the deities in historical inscriptions. More about this will be addressed in Chapter 10 when considering the relationship between the kings and the deities.

A brief survey of what some modern scholars regard as "historiographic" and "historical" documents highlights the role of the deities in these inscriptions.[41] The Sumerian King List states in its opening line that kingship was lowered from heaven, meaning the concept of kingship is a religiously-oriented office. An inscription dating to the reign of Sargon of Agade (2334-2279) begins with Sargon's titles, which include "overseer of Ishtar, anointed priest of Anu, king of the country, great *ensi* of Enlil." The body of the text claims that "Enlil did not let anybody oppose Sargon...."[42]

In the Neo-Assyrian period the Assyrian kings left long detailed accounts of their reigns, and these texts are full of references to what the deities did to allow the kings to succeed. Most of these inscriptions also begin with some comment about how the deities picked them and enabled them to carry out their tasks. Thus, even "historical" inscriptions are used to acknowledge the deities and connect the Mesopotamian kings to their service to their deities.

Conclusions

Despite a wide range of texts that address topics and issues that could be viewed as religious in nature, they reveal really only one basic fundamental

40. Lambert, *Babylonian Wisdom Literature*, 53-56.
41. *ANET,* ix-x.
42. *ANET,* 267.

understanding of humans' role on earth: to serve the deities. The disputations suggest that not only humans but all other objects, animate and inanimate, serve a similar function. Wisdom literature and the historical inscriptions provide insight into an individual's notion of how life is
affecting him or her. Yet even here, the wisdom literature suggests that it is
not humans' place to dictate to the gods. The historical inscriptions, from
the perspective of the kings, imply that kingship is bestowed by the deities
and so kings must do their best to use their power to promote their deity.
Nowhere is there a sense that humans and the world have any particular
direction or are on a path to something or somewhere different or better.
The texts suggest that this is the world populated by humans and gods, and
the role for humans is to figure out how best to appease the gods.

CHAPTER 9

Rituals

R ituals are one of the rare categories where we know something concrete about ancient Mesopotamian religion because the Mesopotamians recorded for themselves how to conduct the rites.[1] As a result, scholars have recovered records of a number of rituals and events such as the
New Year festival, Opening the Mouth of a statue of a deity to animate it,
and the Sacred Marriage. The feeding of the gods and the various pro-
cesses of divination constitute forms of ritual insofar as they are standardized means of caring for the gods and determining what they need. Various rituals often called "magic" will be included here because the activities
of the magician, at least in Mesopotamia, were considered as legitimate as
what priests and other religious personnel were practicing.

Some rituals took place on a daily or regular basis, others happened
yearly, and others were required because of special circumstances. To some
extent, the nature of the ritual is impacted by how often it occurred, which
is sometimes connected to who was present when it took place. This chapter will begin therefore with a brief introduction to the Mesopotamian calendar and then will treat the various categories by whether they took place
more regularly than yearly, yearly, or periodically when necessary.

----

1. A standard definition of a ritual is "a set form or system of rites, religious rites
or otherwise"; *Webster's New World Dictionary: Second Collegiate Edition*, 1229.

Mesopotamian Cycle

Ancient people in general were aware of the regularized shifting cycles of the earth's rotation, in modern times referred to as the calendar. The Mesopotamians recognized the difference between the lengths of the lunar and solar years, though they opted for a lunar cycle. The problem is that some festivals were bound to the solar seasons, though they still received fixed days in a lunar scheme. In order that the lunar calendar remain somewhat in line with the solar calendar, the ancient Mesopotamians intercalated the year, adding an extra month as necessary, to ensure that festivals observed in a particular month coincided with the correct season being celebrated.[2]

Mesopotamians used the moon to calculate months. Each month began at "the moment when, following the period of invisibility due to nearness of the sun, the lunar crescent appears again briefly on the western horizon just after sunset."[3] The month was based on actual sightings of the moon, not predetermined calculations.[4] The Mesopotamians also recognized the cycle between the equinoxes. In Babylonia, the year was divided into two seasons, summer, the hot season, and winter, or the cold season, each beginning in the month of an equinox. This six-month equinox year appears to have been a significant factor in the cultic calendar throughout the Near East, because in many locations there were parallel major festivals in the first and seventh month.[5] The connection between the calendar and the clearly recognized cycles of the year should not be surprising in light of the early date for many of the calendars and rituals and the roots of many ancient Mesopotamian deities in nature.

The relationship between deities, cities, and the pantheon is also apparent in the early calendars. The pre-Sargonic tablets from Lagash indicate that many of the cities in the Lagash city-state had separate calendars, but they shared month names. Despite this complication, already there is a syncretism among the gods of its cities showing a shared observance of major festivals. The texts reveal a community of cities where pilgrimages were taken to observe major festivals in other towns, including offerings

---

2. Cohen, *The Cultic Calendars of the Ancient Near East*, 3.
3. Rochberg-Halton, "Calendars, Ancient Near East," 810.
4. Cohen, *The Cultic Calendars*, 4.
5. Cohen, *The Cultic Calendars*, 6-7.

and pilgrim processions from town to town and shrine to shrine.[6] In typical Mesopotamian fashion, the tablets detail the offerings provided on a daily basis.[7]

The mixture of peoples each with differing calendars — especially in the second millennium when new groups like the Hurrians and Amorites entered Mesopotamia — probably led to the development of the Standard Mesopotamian calendar.[8] It was likely commissioned by Samsuiluna of Babylon as a means of uniting his empire. While this may have helped unify Babylonia, Assyria did not adopt the Standard Mesopotamian calendar until the reign of Tiglath-Pileser I (114-1076). During the reign of Sennacherib, when relations between Assyria and Babylonia were particularly bad, new or foreign month names were introduced into the Assyrian version of the calendar in place of the standard Mesopotamian names used in Babylonia. It may be precisely in this period that the name of Assur replaced Marduk in the *Enuma Elish* in Assyria and thus politics, calendar, and religious worship there were interconnected.

Daily Rituals

The most obvious daily ritual was the feeding of the gods. Since the ancient Mesopotamians believed humans were created to serve the gods, feeding them on a regular basis was maybe one of the more mundane tasks but possibly one of the more important. A detailed text dating to the Seleucid period indicates the divine statues in the temple of Uruk were served two meals a day, the first in the morning when the temple opened and the second at night, immediately before closing the doors of the sanctuary. Each meal had two courses, the "main" and "second," with the difference being one of quantity not content.[9] The meals were served in a style and manner befitting a king. Scholars suggest that the practices described for feeding the divine images also reveal practices in the Babylonian court.[10]

6. Cohen, *The Cultic Calendars*, 9.
7. Cohen, *The Cultic Calendars*, 9.
8. Cohen, *The Cultic Calendars*, 299.
9. Oppenheim, *Ancient Mesopotamia*, 188.
10. Oppenheim, *Ancient Mesopotamia*, 188.

As has been noted, the Mesopotamians may not have explained *why* they did things, but the extant descriptions are detailed regarding *what* they did. A table was brought in and placed before the image, then water for washing was offered, and a number of liquid and semi-liquid dishes were placed on the table in a prescribed arrangement, with beverage containers as well. Specific cuts of meat were served for the main dish followed by fruit, described as a beautiful arrangement. The meal was accompanied by musicians and the cella was fumigated before the table was cleared and removed and water was brought to cleanse the deity's fingers. The meal was clearly fit for a king, because after having been presented to the deity's image the dishes from the god's meal were sent to the king.[11]

Not only did the meal need to be carefully prepared and served, but also the items to be used in the meal involved appropriate acts. Special blessings were pronounced at numerous times in the processing of any of the items to be served. For the bread alone there were prayers for when barley was ground for the sacrificial bread, when the baker was kneading the dough, and when the loaves were taken from the oven.[12]

Despite the extreme attention to the preparation and presentation of the offerings to the deity, humans were not allowed to watch the deity consume the presentation. The deity's image and the table with the deity's food were surrounded by linen curtains during the meal and when the deity was washing. Oppenheim speculates that this tradition developed because of the mysterious nature of the assimilation of the food by the image.[13] Again, because we know so little about how the ancient Mesopotamians felt about the images of their deities and how they interfaced with them, it is unclear whether or not they considered the fact that the food was not somehow actually consumed by the image to be problematic.

Yearly Rituals

The festival cycles in Mesopotamia and agricultural life are interconnected already in the third millennium B.C.E. Observances marked the grain har-

11. Oppenheim, *Ancient Mesopotamia,* 188-89.
12. Oppenheim, *Ancient Mesopotamia,* 191.
13. Oppenheim, *Ancient Mesopotamia,* 192.

vest, plowing and planting seasons, making of malt, and gathering in of fall produce, though the records detailing what was performed and what was said at each of these vary over time and place.[14] As in other aspects of Mesopotamian life, there was a shift from each city having its own cultic calendar to much more homogenization in the first millennium.

Perhaps the most important Mesopotamian yearly festivals were the *Akītu* festivals, particularly the one marking the New Year. Its importance is apparent in that it is one of the oldest recorded Mesopotamian festivals, referred to already in the Fara period in the mid-third millennium.[15] Here too, how and when this festival was celebrated changed over time and place. It is also the case that the meaning for the festival varied from place to place. The reasons for the shifts were, at times, politically motivated, at least from our later vantage point. Rather than survey how the *Akītu* festival was celebrated at all times and in all places, we will address such basic aspects as when the festival was celebrated, what and who were involved, and what special items were needed for it. A focus on how the festival was conducted in one particular place in a certain period will shed light on how and why various components of the festival evolved.

The Mesopotamian cultic calendar was influenced by the cycles of the moon, the seasons, and the equinoxes. The *Akītu* festivals, observed primarily in the first and seventh months, marked the six-month equinox throughout the ancient Near East.[16] In some places there were parallel major festivals in the first and seventh months, indicating two new years rather than treating the autumnal *Akītu* as the sole New Year, as best known from Babylon in the first millennium.

The association of the New Year with the autumnal equinox in the seventh month is likely rooted in Mesopotamian mythology and reflects the importance of Ur in the third millennium. Ur appears to be the original site of the *Akītu* festival, where the observance is referenced already in pre-Sargonic texts.[17] Since there it was a semi-annual event, the *Akītu* in Ur was not a celebration of the New Year of the seasonal cycle but of the equinoxes and so was fixed to the months in which the vernal and autumnal equinoxes usually occurred: the first and seventh months. Though

14. Cohen, *The Cultic Calendars,* 389.
15. Cohen, *The Cultic Calendars,* 401.
16. Cohen, *The Cultic Calendars,* 400.
17. Cohen, *The Cultic Calendars,* 401.

these events are not necessarily tied to the first day of the lunar month, since the festival marked the beginning of the equinox, apparently it was natural that the Mesopotamians would associate it with the new moon.[18] The autumnal equinox in the seventh month marks the beginning of the time when the moon was visible longer than the sun. Ur's patron deity being Nanna, the moon-deity, for the inhabitants of that city it is not surprising that the *Akītu* festival celebrated in the seventh month became more important than that of the first month and thus was considered the beginning of the New Year.[19]

This tradition became set, and for most places in most periods the first and seventh months were the primary time for *Akītu* festivals, with the New Year festival occurring in the seventh month.[20] However, in some cities *Akītu* festivals were held in other months. For example, the festival was celebrated in the fourth and twelfth months in third-millennium Nippur and Adab and at Uruk in the eighth month.[21]

A number of ancient texts, some more thorough than others, document what took place on each day of the *Akītu* festivals in different periods of Mesopotamian history. In general, the *Akītu* in the first month lasted approximately five days, while the celebration in the seventh month, which became the New Year festival, lasted eleven days.[22]

For Babylon a day-by-day account of the autumn New Year festival can be reconstructed from ritual texts, commentaries, and historical inscriptions, though gaps remain.[23] On the fourth day morning prayers were offered to Bel and his consort in the Esagil, followed by the blessing of the temple. After the evening meal the high priest recited the *Enuma Elish* to Marduk, followed by a procession from the Ezida temple in Borsippa to the Ezida chapel in the Esagil complex in Babylon, where the statue of Nabu, Marduk's son, entered the city. Other events, for different days, include ritual slaughter of sheep, the high priest striking the king's cheek (presumably to instill within the king the feeling of penitence) and dragging him before Marduk where the king knelt like a servant, swearing to

18. Cohen, *The Cultic Calendars*, 401.
19. Cohen, *The Cultic Calendars*, 402.
20. Cohen, *The Cultic Calendars*, 406-53.
21. Cohen, *The Cultic Calendars*, 415.
22. Cohen, *The Cultic Calendars*, 402.
23. Cohen, *The Cultic Calendars*, 437.

Marduk that he had not sinned against Babylon and had fulfilled his obligations, gods celebrating at the *akītu*-house, and the gods assembling to determine destiny.[24]

The interaction with the king is particularly significant and may be at the heart of the ritual. After the king swore to Marduk that he had not sinned, the priest again struck the king's cheek, and if tears flowed, then Marduk had accepted him; but if tears did not flow, Marduk would have the king overthrown.[25] This ritual thus associates the triumphal return of the deity to the city with the performance review of the king of the city. The importance of this ritual for the city, both ritually and politically, highlights the importance of some events in Babylon's history. For example, during the ten-year absence of King Nabonidus, the ritual could not be performed. Not only could the god Marduk not reveal his triumphant role in the *Enuma Elish* during those years, thus legitimating his position in the pantheon, but the king's performance could not be evaluated by his patron, Marduk.

The program for the ritual is connected in a number of ways with the purpose of the festival, which also evolved over time. The summary of events in first-millennium Babylon differs significantly from that for the festival's origins when Marduk was but a minor player. When the observance originated in Ur, it was a festival of the moon, to celebrate the equinoxes, highlighting Nanna's triumphant entry to his city.[26] The pageantry of the event became associated with the deity's assumption of control of the city as reenacted at the festival. When other cities adopted the festival and adapted it for their own city-gods, deities not necessarily associated with the moon, the association with the equinox completely disappeared. With the creation of the *Enuma Elish* and its association with the rise of Marduk and the city of Babylon and its king, the festival evolved even further.

While the position of Marduk as hero and champion of Babylon is clear, the *Akītu* festival and Marduk's role took a very different path in Assyria. Whether an *Akītu* festival can be traced in Assyria as early as the Old Assyrian period is subject to debate, but there is a clearly attested ritual at Assur dating to between the reign of Tukulti-Ninurta I and the return of

24. Cohen, *The Cultic Calendars,* 438-39.
25. Cohen, *The Cultic Calendars,* 438.
26. Cohen, *The Cultic Calendars,* 453.

Marduk to his residence during the reign of Ninurta-tukul-Assur (ca. 1350-1250). In this ritual, the king presented gifts to the gods, and then the king, the *sangu* priest, and the statues of the other gods stood before Marduk as the god sat on the Throne of Destiny.[27] Note that Marduk was not the main deity of Assyria but of Babylon, the city Tukulti-Ninurta destroyed.

An Assyrian ritual commentary suggests a mythological background to the *Akītu* festival in Assyria, different than the one posited for the New Year in Ur. According to this commentary, Marduk transgressed against the god Assur and was imprisoned in the *akītu* house, where he underwent trial by ordeal before being released. Apparently, Marduk's crime was his claim to supremacy over the gods, a major focus of the *Enuma Elish*, the text read at the New Year festival. Another charge leveled at Marduk concerns the "wearing of the water." This suggests that Assur claims that he was the one who defeated Tiamat and that Marduk was only pretending to take the victory. Assur claims that, in fact, Marduk had not even come into existence at the time of the battle and thus could not have defeated Tiamat. In the extant Assyrian versions of *Enuma Elish*, the name of Assur appears instead of Marduk. Thus, in Assyria, Assur is the triumphant deity and identifies Marduk as a criminal, detaining him in the *akītu*-house. The *akītu*-house, which in other instances represented a temporary residence for Marduk before claiming residence in his new city, therefore became a temporary jail for him in Assur and Nineveh.[28] Upon his release after seven days he does not, as in the other instances, march triumphantly into his new city.

As noted above, there are likely political reasons behind the modifications of the ritual and/or infusing it with new meaning. Tukulti-Ninurta I was one of the Assyrian kings who defeated Babylon and captured Marduk in the process. While the statue of Marduk was detained in Assyria, the Assyrians took responsibility for maintaining the cult of the captured deity and performing the *Akītu* festival. While they maintained the ritual, clearly it was provided new meaning.

---

27. Cohen, *The Cultic Calendars*, 419-20.
28. Cohen, *The Cultic Calendars*, 420.

Other Rituals

Sacred Marriage

One of the more frequently mentioned rituals, but one difficult to understand, was the Sacred Marriage. This is suggested to have been an event when the earthly king reenacted the sexual union representing the official moment of marriage between the king and a female divine figure, usually Inanna/Ishtar. Scholars have long debated whether this was reenacted using an actual person, like a high priestess, or symbolically, with a statue of a divine female. Much of the discussion is based on a number of early texts and the stories concerning Dumuzi and Ishtar. More recently, the notion of a "sacred marriage" as an actual physical union between the king and a person or image representing the divine female has changed significantly from a physical event conducted on New Year's Day to a metaphorical union.

"Sacred marriage" is a technical term in the study of religion for a mythical or ritual union between a divine and human being, usually a king and a goddess. In Mesopotamia in general, the term is applied to the intimate relationship between the goddess Inanna and the king, as described in the Dumuzi-Inanna love songs. The king is identified by his proper name or referred to as Dumuzi, an antediluvian king and Inanna's mythical lover. Though some are earlier, most of the texts come from the Ur III period, from Shulgi into the following Isin era.[29]

There is little agreement among Mesopotamian scholars as to the point of such a union. The main proposals cover a wide range and include fertility, coronation, legitimization of kingship involving deification of the king, obtaining blessings for the king, producing an heir for the throne, installation of *en* or *nin-dingir* priestesses, practicing the *en*-ship of Inanna, secular love songs, and love songs as royal or court poetry.[30] The problem with understanding precisely what is involved in the actual ritual is that the language of most of the texts is explicitly sexual and appears to describe a physical union between the king and the goddess Inanna, but never do the texts address why this may be. Because there is little agreement about why the ritual was conducted, there is also little consensus as

29. Lapinkivi, *The Sumerian Sacred Marriage*, 1-2.
30. Lapinkivi (3-14) provides a thorough list of the main reasons for the various proposals as well as the scholars who argued for them.

to whether the king actually had sex with a priestess playing the part of the goddess or whether such references suggest a symbolic union. Note too the difference from other rituals for which texts survive detailing what to do and when.

Further complicating our understanding of the Sacred Marriage is that the ritual is attested in Sumer but, as most scholars agree, this early ritual ended by the time of Hammurabi of Babylon when there is an influx of a new group to the region, the Amorites. The Sacred Marriage appears to resurface in the first millennium, but in a form that has changed dramatically, even to the extent that the participants are no longer Inanna and Dumuzi but Nabu and Tashmetu or Nanaya, Marduk and Zarpanitu joined with Ishtar, Shamash, and Aya, and Anu and Antu.[31] There is little interconnecting textual evidence between the Sacred Marriage of the third millennium and that of the first, although later love song catalogues include references to the Sumerian songs.[32] Note too, as will be seen in the next chapter, the Ur III kings were deified in their lifetimes, and thus the changed nature of the earthly king may have led to changes in the need for or point of the ritual.

The available sources suggest that, while the marriage of Inanna and Dumuzi was celebrated at least on New Year's Day, it could also be performed monthly, possibly on the last day of the month, the "day of the disappearance of the moon." The evidence for the timing of the Sacred Marriage is found in only two of the Dumuzi/Inanna songs, and these references date to the early form of the rite. The timing of the first millennium Sacred Marriage varies significantly. For example, in the Assurbanipal hymn, the marriage takes place monthly, but two letters suggest the marriage of Nabu and Tashmetu happened in the month of Ayyaru (April-May).[33] This should not be too surprising, since in this context there are different couples taking part.

The references to, gap in observance, and uncertain nature of the Sacred Marriage reflect the ebb and flow of Mesopotamian religion. What precisely constituted the Sacred Marriage in third-millennium Sumer is clearly not what it was in the first millennium. The connection is difficult to determine, and scholars cannot agree either on the ritual's original

---

31. Lapinkivi, *The Sumerian Sacred Marriage*, 81.
32. Lapinkivi, *The Sumerian Sacred Marriage*, 14.
33. Lapinkivi, *The Sumerian Sacred Marriage*, 245-46.

meaning or its continuation with a radically different purpose and procedure later in history.

Mīs pî

The *mīs pî* ritual, which best translates as "opening of the mouth," was a purificatory rite which prepared the object or person for contact with the divine.[34] While the ritual could be performed in a number of settings, in its most sacred context it transformed a piece of stone into a cult image. Since cult images were not created on a regular basis but at special times, the ritual was never standardized, so it was not as tied to a calendar as other rites. Many modern scholars consider this the most solemn, sacred, and secret of Mesopotamian rituals because it called upon all the knowledge and spiritual know-how of the ritual specialists to bring the deity from the spiritual realm to the physical.[35]

The *mīs pî* ritual could be performed on items other than cult statues. It could be performed in royal rituals involving either the king or his royal insignia, in which, for example, the king spits on a statue and then washes his mouth with water and beer. Animals and sacred objects could have their mouths washed, as could an ordinary human, a god, and priests. The goal of the ritual was to wash away impurities. It is possible that the ritual may have originated in the need for the priest's having clean breath when he approached the deity, since he was cautioned to keep away from odiferous foods like leeks and fish. What began as an attempt to protect the deity from bad breath may then have led to a concern for total purity.[36]

Other cult images could also have their mouths opened. Some rituals used apotropaic figurines to which a threatening evil could be transferred, and opening of the mouth would enliven the figurine so that it would function as a substitute either for the sick person, the king, or the king's enemy. Other objects whose "mouth" could be opened include a leather-bag, cult symbols, a river (to restore order to its waters), and jewels to protect the king's chariot.[37] This may all sound odd today, but the

---

34. Walker and Dick, *The Induction of the Cult Image,* paraphrasing Boden.
35. Walker and Dick, *The Induction of the Cult Image,* 12.
36. Walker and Dick, *The Induction of the Cult Image,* 10-12.
37. Walker and Dick, *The Induction of the Cult Image,* 13.

point was to allow the object to become more than just an object, almost to transform it.

There is not much evidence for the development of this ritual over time, since the earliest example dates only to Nabu-apla-iddina in the ninth century B.C.E. There is, however, a reference to the mouth-opening of a statue of Gudea of Lagash as well as Sumerian incantations which some attribute to the opening of the mouth of a statue.[38] It appears then that the ritual was part of Mesopotamian tradition from the third millennium, but without much data it is difficult to assess how or why it evolved over time.

Scholars classify the *mīs pî* as a major Mesopotamian cultic ritual of considerable complexity. The action is spread over one or more days, with instructions written on a numbered series of tablets, and the text of the incantations given in full. As such, quite a few details are known about what takes place. Included are preparations in the city, countryside, and temple, a procession from the workshop to the river, events at the riverbank, procession from the riverbank into the orchard, rituals within the circle of reed-huts in the orchard, another procession from the orchard to the gate of the temple followed by a procession from the gate to the holy of holies, with additional rituals in each of those places.[39]

Such elaborate ritual underscores the importance of the event. Since humans were created to serve the gods, and the purpose of the city and its administration is to service the god, creating an appropriate cult image of the deity for the city could not be taken lightly. The *mīs pî* ritual served many purposes. It secured the image's purity. In order for the image to reflect the deity, all traces of the work of the human craftsman had to disappear for the supernatural origin of the image to prevail. The Mesopotamians recognized that before the ritual the image did not have senses, and the *mīs pî* activated them. Through the ritual the image was also brought into the community of its divine companions and was led into its realm and home, the temple.[40]

It is impossible to cover every ritual preserved from ancient Mesopotamia, and the examples brought in here are some of the major and most famous. Yet it is important to remember that there were numerous rituals

38. Walker and Dick, *The Induction of the Cult Image*, 18.
39. Walker and Dick, *The Induction of the Cult Image*, 29-30.
40. Walker and Dick, *The Induction of the Cult Image*, 30.

for a whole range of other circumstances. For example, animal sacrifice required specific requirements to ensure that the ritual quality of the animal was preserved, and we have fairly detailed information preserved on an Old Babylonian bilingual text with instructions for the butchering, preparation, and inspection of a sacrificial sheep.[41] For the ancient Mesopotamians, the details of ritual were important.

Magic

A category that many would not consider religious ritual, but in the Mesopotamian context should be, is what is often described as "magic." In antiquity, and often in the modern world, magic refers to someone else's religious practice. Magic was almost always a normative rather than a descriptive term, so it is difficult to make a clean division between it and religion. Since there are few substantive differences between "magic" and "religion," some rituals that might be considered magical will be considered here.[42]

Ancient Mesopotamia had no category considered "magic" that was clearly distinguished from anything that could be viewed as religious. Magic was simply regarded as a normal aspect of life and was not disapproved.[43] What will be addressed as "magic" here are those spells and counterspells (releases) that were intended to rescue humans from the easily-provoked deities.

Two major forms of magic were practiced: black and white. Black magic, often labeled "sorcery," brought harm to people and was regarded as evil because of its social effects, though it may have used the same methods as standard (white) magic.[44] White magic sought to turn away evil caused by demons, malevolent powers, and humans.[45] Most of the preserved tablets describe white magical activities.

Since the ancient Mesopotamians were never sure precisely what their deities wanted or expected, and the deities, as the Mesopotamians under-

---

41. Foxvog, "A Manual of Sacrificial Procedure," 167.
42. Johnston, "Magic," 139-40.
43. Black and Green, "Magic and Sorcery," in *Gods, Demons and Symbols,* 124.
44. Black and Green, "Magic and Sorcery," 125.
45. Nemet-Nejat, *Daily Life,* 197.

Clay liver model, inscribed with omens and magical formulas (1st Dynasty of Babylon, ca. 1830-1550 B.C.E.). *(Courtesy, The British Museum)*

stood them, changed their minds frequently and were moody, any kind of demon or supernatural force could threaten anyone at any time for any reason. For example, an individual could commit a sin unknowingly,[46] resulting in a ban or a curse that would cause him to be alienated from the favor of the god(s), usually resulting in sickness. When the sufferer realized he had sinned, he could remedy the situation, but if the reason for divine anger remained unclear, he would need to resort to magic.[47]

Among the most common forms of magic were incantations or spells. These were "systematic descriptions" (therefore rituals), addressed to the

46. See above, 98-99, on the "wisdom" text, Poem of the Righteous Sufferer; Lambert, *Babylonian Wisdom Literature*, 21-62.

47. Nemet-Nejat, *Daily Life*, 197.

magician, of the actions to be employed, including a list of the incantations to be uttered at specific points, either by the magician or the patient. Amulets inscribed with excerpts from appropriate incantations were worn around the neck or hung on the wall of a house. Apotropaic figurines were also used.[48]

Incantations originated as responses to individual cases and were later gathered into compendia. The earliest incantations preserved date from the Early Dynastic period and appear to protect against snake-bite and scorpions, to assist in childbirth, or to consecrate objects used in magical rituals. By the Old Babylonian Period the individual Sumerian incantations were already grouped together according to their function or the demons they were intended to protect against.[49] This led to the compilation of two handbooks, *Shurpu* and *Maqlū,* each having a particular purpose. *Shurpu* was a collection of spells and rituals that described the types of misbehavior so the person who committed these deeds could be purified through appropriate rites. These misbehaviors included cultic negligence, domestic trouble, uncharitable conduct, cruelty to animals, and unintentional contact with ritually unclean people or places. *Maqlū* was concerned with burning the image of a witch by fire to negate its powers. In both cases it is important to identify the perpetrator.[50] Another series, *Namburbu,* contained incantations intended to undo or avert the effect of future evil detected in advance by means of portents.

Many of these rituals are carefully recorded. As with those discussed above, the texts do not necessarily explain how the various components remedy the situation, but they do describe in fairly full detail the steps involved in the ritual. For example, most of the *Namburbu* rituals involve a sequence of five rites. These include isolating the ritual from the outside world, purifiying the patient, offering food and aromatics to the gods, more purification, then returning the patient to the outside world.[51]

For the ancient Mesopotamians, the need for magic is completely "religious" insofar as it stems from their understanding of the nature of the universe. The world was controlled by gods whom people were created to serve. It was not always clear what the gods needed or demanded, and so

48. Black and Green, "Magic and Sorcery," 126.
49. Black and Green, "Magic and Sorcery," 126.
50. Nemet-Nejat, *Daily Life,* 197.
51. Black and Green, "Magic and Sorcery," 126-27.

when something negative befell a person, it was viewed as coming from the gods. Determining precisely what happened and how to resolve it demanded a special category of specialists trained in a specific field, supported by a body of literature. The "cure" involved a series of rites employing specific texts, a broad definition of ritual. Because one never knew when bad things might befall a person, there was no systematic timetable for these rituals to be performed. All of this ties in neatly with the Mesopotamian worldview expressed in each of the other areas considered thus far.

Conclusions

Rituals were important to the ancient Mesopotamians. They were performed on a regular basis and whenever special circumstances demanded them. Most of the major rituals originated in the earliest recorded periods of Mesopotamian history and evolved over time. The importance of the rituals is clear from the precise recording of how they were to be conducted.

CHAPTER 10

Kingship, Religion, and the Gods

B ecause the relationship between the Mesopotamian kings and the deities is significant, it is treated here as a separate topic. If people were on earth to provide for the gods, then the main function and justification of the state was to supply what was necessary for the gods. The cult, under the supervision of the ruler, had to meet this obligation. As a result, the relationship of the ruler to the gods was unique and foundational for the state. The important relationship between the gods and the kings developed early in Mesopotamian history. The original rulers of the Sumerian city-states were more priestlike than kinglike, or at least that role was more heavily emphasized. Such was the case through the end of Babylonian history, where annual review of the rulers at the *Akītu* festival was conducted by the high priest and the deity as part of the New Year festival.

This chapter will explore the nuances of the relationship of the ancient Mesopotamian kings with the deities. After first exploring the general nature of this relationship and where and how it was expressed, we will then consider the few cases of overt deification of ancient Mesopotamian kings.

The King's Relationship with the Divine

In a discussion about kingship and divinity, Irene Winter begins with a general conclusion whose importance is appropriate here:

The Mesopotamian ruler was *never not* accorded special status sanctioned by the gods. From earliest attestations, he participated in and was touched by the divine, and so occupied a space, if not co-terminus with that of a god, then at least that of an intermediary between god and man.[1]

While the relationship between the Mesopotamian rulers and their deities may vary, as well as which deities they served or promoted and when and how they did so, the notion that the kings held a special relationship with the divine did not change.

Much discussion about the relationship of rulers to the deities focuses on the early periods of Mesopotamian history because it is in the third millennium that the clearest examples of divinized earthly kings are attested. Nevertheless, the relationship between the ruler and the deities was of paramount importance and differed from that between other mortals and the deities. Some now argue that the idea that there were only two states of existence in the ancient world, mortal/human and divine, is a reflection of our "Aristotelian-based scientific classification system" and that we need to reconsider our categories.[2] In fact, this concept flies in the face of Mesopotamian literature, with the simple examples of Gilgamesh and his good friend Enkidu, both of whom the text presents as composite beings, both divine and human.[3]

The connection between the divine and kingship, and therefore to the actual kings themselves, is articulated by the Sumerians in the idea that kingship is a physical matter that is lowered from heaven. This is stated explicitly throughout the Sumerian King List, including the first line: "When kingship was lowered from heaven. . . ."[4] Although most scholars understand the Sumerian King List to be a work produced by the rulers of Isin to justify their taking over the Ur III state, this does not diminish the impor-

1. Winter, "Touched by the Gods," 75.

2. Selz, "The Divine Prototypes," 13-14.

3. For the composite nature of Gilgamesh, see the Epic of Gilgamesh, tablet ii line 1: "Two-thirds of him is god, [one third of him is human]"; *ANET,* 73. For the combined nature of Enkidu, see Gilgamesh, tablet ii lines 33-34: "A double of Anu she conceived within her. Arura washed her hands, Pinched off clay and cast it on the steppe"; *ANET,* 74.

4. Jacobsen, *The Sumerian King List,* 71.

tance of the concept. The rhetoric would not be effective without the notion that kingship was somehow divinely justified and promoted.

While kingship may have been a divine office, the kings, normally, were not regarded as such. The concept of kingship and the powers of the office were fairly consistent in Mesopotamia. Such an important office came with clear responsibilities including advising his people, overseeing labor, building and administering cities, protecting the land, providing abundance, and performing ritual services to the gods. Despite the continuity in terms of what the kings were required to do, how they functioned in their community and the accoutrements of that role changed over time and place.[5]

In the pre-Sargonic periods, the specific function of the king was not as precise as it later came to be, yet there are clues concerning his role and therefore his relationship to the divine. The Sumerian word for king is *lugal,* which means "big man." Both texts and images of some of these early kings, such as Eannatum of Lagash, suggest that the king was both larger in scale and in filial relationship to the gods, implying his status as somehow "higher" than that of regular humans.[6]

Beginning with Naram-Sin, the third millennium produced kings who declared themselves actual divinities. Yet even those who did not make such claims maintained close ties to the divine. For example, Gudea of Lagash refers to the goddess Nanshe as his "mother" and states that he had been selected for rule because he was physically outstanding and his personal god Ningishzida made his "head stand out in the assembly." Proof of this was claimed in texts which declared his physical qualities as gifts of specific gods, such as the breadth of his chest and full-muscled arm. Many of these physical attributes were also manifested in sculptural representations of the ruler, so text and image together represent Gudea as more than merely human.[7]

During the Isin/Larsa and Old Babylonian periods, the focus of the king's service to the gods was on cultic service and temple-building, as suggested in foundation cones and royal hymns.[8] In the preface to his famous

---

5. Numerous examples demonstrate how the king's relationship with the deity is manifested throughout Mesopotamian history. Art historian Winter has considered both the textual and visual evidence, and her examples will be the focus here; "Touched by the Gods," 75-101.

6. Winter, "Touched by the Gods," 80-81.

7. Winter, "Touched by the Gods," 81.

8. Winter, "Touched by the Gods," 82.

law code, Hammurabi proclaims that he was called ("named") by the gods to rule and to "rise like the god Shamash over all humankind."[9] In the epilogue, he claims humankind has been granted to his care by the god Enlil, "with whose shepherding the god Marduk charged me." This he was able to do with the mighty weapon bestowed upon him by the gods Zababa and Ishtar, the wisdom from Ea, and the ability given him by Marduk.[10] The visual imagery reinforces Hammurabi's authority to promulgate law. The small image at the top of the stela portrays Hammurabi standing before the seated sun-god Shamash. Here Hammurabi makes direct eye contact with the deity, and the king's head is slightly higher than the deity's, presenting the two almost as equals.[11] Thus, Hammurabi receives verbal permission from a range of deities for his reign, legitimating his laws, and this is reinforced visually by his stature in front of the god of justice.

A special divine relationship between the gods and kings is also apparent in Assyria. Scholars have noted an increase in the textual rhetoric claiming a close connection of the king to the gods in the reign of Tukulti-Ninurta I. The king's body is described as the flesh of the gods, and there are references to a radiant aura surrounding the ruler.[12] While the language used to associate the ruler with divine authorization is slightly different, the concept that the kings have a special relationship with the gods continues to manifest itself.

Later Assyrian kings also identify themselves closely with the divine. Adad-Nirari II declares that the gods perfected his features, marking him as fit to rule. In a letter to Esarhaddon, one writer claims that in his perfection the monarch is the "perfect likeness of the god." Some texts go so far as to equate the kings with gods, as in a hymn supposedly composed for Assurbanipal's coronation, where the ruler is stated to be the sun(-god). Another text describing the Assyrian king going to battle claims, "the king who stands in the chariot is the warrior king, the Lord (god) Ninurta."[13] Scholars focusing on the Neo-Assyrian period point out that the question of the divinity of kings in that era has not received as much attention as for other periods. They note that the issue is quite complex and the divine sta-

9. Roth, *Law Collections from Mesopotamia and Asia Minor*, 76-77.
10. Roth, *Law Collections*, 133.
11. Winter, "Touched by the Gods," 83.
12. Winter, "Touched by the Gods," 83-84.
13. Winter, "Touched by the Gods," 84-85.

Stela depicting Hammurabi receiving symbols of authority from the sun-god Shamash. Below are listed 282 laws exemplifying the ideals of royal justice. *(Louvre)*

tus of kings had its limits.[14] Yet for purposes here, the key issue is that the Neo-Assyrian kings, like the Babylonian kings, claimed they had a special relationship with the gods, leading them to have special divine abilities and authorization for their rule.

Divine Kings

Only a few Mesopotamian kings claimed divine status during their life-times. While these cases are important, it is nevertheless noteworthy that they are only a few. As noted, the divinity of the ancient Mesopotamian

14. Winter, "Touched by the Gods," 80-81. Also Holloway, *Assur Is King! Assur Is King!*, 178.

kings came through divine favor bestowed upon them, not in their being fully divine. In general, recent scholarship treats the few examples of divine kings, like most other components of ancient Mesopotamian religion, as historically defined phenomena rather than as moments in a developmental trajectory.

The earliest Mesopotamian king to claim divine status was Naram-Sin, the grandson of Sargon of Akkad. Since the site of Akkad has not been archaeologically identified, we have no texts recording this event. His divine status is suggested because he is identified with the divine classifier *d* (*dingir,* "god") written before his name and he is depicted artistically with the horned crown usually reserved for deities. Only one explicit contemporary text survives that refers to Naram-Sin's elevation to the status of a deity:

> Because he secured the foundations of his city (Agade) in times of trouble, his city requested of Ishtar in Eana, of Enlil in Nippur, of Dagan in Tuttul, of Ninhursanga in Kesh, of Ea in Eridu, of Sin in Ur, of Shamash in Sippar, and of Nergal in Kutha, that (Naram-Sin) be made a god, and then built his temple in the midst of (the city of) Agade.[15]

The context of this action and its specific claims are necessary to understand the place of the deification of rulers in Mesopotamia. According to this sole inscription, the initiation of the action is not attributed to the king. Rather, he claims that the citizens of the city requested it. In fact, his deification appears as a reward for saving the state.[16] According to the inscription, the people's request was approved by all the major deities of the kingdom. Finally, Naram-Sin was not made god of the entire region but only of the city of Akkad, and he presumably joined Ishtar-Annunitum as the divine city ruler, and maybe even her consort. There is no further textual information about a cult of Naram-Sin. Texts referring to Naram-Sin's reign following his deification indicate that he dedicated himself to supporting the cults of other deities in cities under his reign, which he apparently had not done earlier in his reign.[17]

15. Michalowski, "Mortal Kings of Ur," 34.

16. This is the occurrence of the phrase "secured the foundations." It became a major ideological concept depicting the security of the state and crown in both Sumerian and Akkadian; Michalowski, "Mortal Kings of Ur," 34.

17. Michalowski, "Mortal Kings of Ur," 34.

Naram-Sin's rule as a deity apparently was not hereditary because his son and successor, Sharkalisharri, does not seem to have claimed the status. Whether Sharkalisharri's name was written with the divine classifier is complicated by the work of Mesopotamian copyists of his texts and modern efforts at restoring breaks. Sharkalisharri's inscriptions include no contemporary year names written with the divine classifier, but two contemporary monuments have it (five do not), as do three contemporary seals (eleven do not).[18] Some scholars apparently assumed divinity was inherited and "restored" the divine classifier in broken passages recording Sharkalisharri's year names.[19] Apparently then, Naram-Sin's status as a divinity constituted only a brief moment during his reign, attributed as a direct response to some accomplishment, and was not passed on to his successors.

Shulgi is the other third-millennium king who was deified. Although Shulgi is now famous for restructuring the Ur III state, in early studies of Mesopotamian history many of his accomplishments were attributed to his father Ur-Namma (previously written Ur-Nammu). The confusion may be related partly to the reasons why Shulgi was deified.

Ur-Namma was mortally wounded while leading troops in battle. Only one other Mesopotamian king, Sargon II of Assyria, is recorded as dying in battle. Violent royal death implied sin and divine abandonment of the ruler and his city. Evidence of the gravity of the situation is a long poem detailing the king's death, journey, and reception in the netherworld, the only such piece of Sumerian literature.[20]

Shulgi responded to the disaster by spending the first twenty years of his reign in extensive cultic, ceremonial, and organizational activity in order to secure the foundations of his rule and so overcome the ideological crisis. Regardless of whatever other significant events may actually have taken place, the years were named after cultic activities and concern the central ceremonial cities of the state, with the exception of years ten and eleven, which claim control of strategic border towns.[21]

18. Michalowski suggests that the count of contemporary seals may actually not reflect so much his status as divine as the work of some of Sharkalisharri's "more enthusiastic servants," since these are dedicatory inscriptions. Michalowski, "Mortal Kings of Ur," 35.

19. Michalowski, "Mortal Kings of Ur," 35.

20. Michalowski, "Mortal Kings of Ur," 35-36.

21. Michalowski, "Mortal Kings of Ur," 36.

All of this changed in year twenty-one, after which almost all of the documents commemorate military expeditions. Possibly more important for purposes here, beginning with year twenty-one Shulgi's name is preceded by the cuneiform sign for "god," which informs readers that Shulgi is divine.[22] Shulgi's deification differed from Naram-Sin's in that he was worshipped in temples and was incorporated into Ur III literature as a brother to Gilgamesh.[23] Shulgi supported the scribal schools, which not only taught the necessary writing skills but also indoctrinated scribes with the ideological aspirations of the Ur III state. As a result, in Ur writing was the instrument by which the crown exercised oversight and control, as documented by the hundred thousand or so published administrative documents from the period.[24]

As noted in Chapter 3 on history, Shulgi's reforms in the re-creation of the Ur III state led to a homogenization of the state and a unity previously not seen in ancient Mesopotamia. This political configuration included the state bureaucracy, taxes, weights and measures, schools, and distribution of goods and services. As a result of Shulgi's deification, the power of the crown was infused into the social, cultural, and economic sphere of the temples, which in the third millennium prior to Shulgi had been large fiscal organizations.[25] All of this displaced the ideational core of the region, which had been anchored in the city, the temple, and the city ruler.[26] Shulgi's appropriation of divine attributes was but one element in this elaborate constellation of activities that constituted a virtual reinvention of his state. Hence his divine status had nothing to do with any autonomous symbolic system: it was but one component in a complex fabric of economic, structural, and ideological reformations that took place in a concrete historical context.[27]

Shulgi's sons and direct descendants had their own temples and were also designated by the cuneiform sign for divinity, ending with Ibbi-Sin, Ur's last ruler, who was taken in chains to Anshan in Elam. According to Mesopotamian tradition, at this point kingship passed over to Isin and its

---

22. Michalowski, "Mortal Kings of Ur," 36.
23. Michalowski, "Mortal Kings of Ur," 37.
24. Michalowski, "Mortal Kings of Ur," 37.
25. Michalowski, "Mortal Kings of Ur," 37.
26. Michalowski, "Charisma and Control," 55.
27. Michalowski, "Mortal Kings of Ur," 37.

king Ishbi-Irra, who had played a large role in the demise of the Ur III state. As a result, the reign of divine kings of Ur lasted only sixty years.

While there has been a great deal of discussion about deified rulers in these two short periods in third-millennium Mesopotamia, it should be noted that in a more than two-thousand-year history their role is relatively minor. Furthermore, political and historical circumstances provide the context for how and why this came about, possibly explaining why they were such unique occurrences.

Conclusions

As with so many other aspects of religion discussed in this volume, the status and relationship of the Mesopotamian rulers changed over time and place. In the third millennium the few instances of divine kings were short-lived moments directly related to the historical and political events of the day. This does not mean that other kings lacked a close relationship to the divine, only that no other king sought deification. References to most Mesopotamian kings in other periods suggest that the relationship between these rulers and their deities was closer than for others among the populace; or, at least it was important to the rulers to portray their relationship as such. The kings boasted about this in a wide range of inscriptions.[28] The New Year festival in Babylon became an important moment in which the king's relationship with the deity, and therefore his authority to rule, was publicly reviewed. This is not surprising, since the justification of the state, and therefore the evaluation of the ruler, is based on the ruler's ability to shepherd his people to best fulfill their role on earth: service to the gods.

28. See "Historical Inscriptions" in Chapter 8.

CHAPTER 11

Conclusions

The goal for this volume has been to introduce students to the religion of ancient Mesopotamia. As explained in the Introduction, the idea was to survey the basic tools available for such study and the major issues surrounding the topic. It was never the goal to cover everything in the field comprehensively.

Despite the preliminary and introductory nature of the enterprise, a number of issues have been thoroughly addressed. It should be clear, when approaching a topic as vast as the religion of an area that spanned a great deal of space and more than two thousand years, with numerous peoples entering the region at different times, bringing in new languages and customs, that change would occur. Despite these rather significant shifts in language, customs, practices, and texts, certain elements of their religion did remain the same.

The key component to understanding most of Mesopotamian religion is the relationship between humans and their deities. In the Mesopotamian view of the world, expressed in a wide range of their texts and manifest in their rituals, temples, and religious personnel, people were on earth to serve the gods. What and how that service should be carried out is what many ancient scholars, religious personnel, kings, and others strove to understand through various means.

While this fundamental principle manifests itself in a number of ways, what is more difficult to determine is how the ancient Mesopotamians felt about any of this. As has been noted repeatedly, they rarely explained why they carried out their actions or what they experienced by doing so. As a result, what many readers may be missing in this discussion is any evidence of the Mesopotamians' emotions behind their religious activities.

The reason for this missing component is not only that the Mesopotamians seldom provide it, but that religious fervor is complicated and difficult to assess. In the modern world, there are numerous ways that adherents of various religions express their devotion. What is appealing and attractive about one approach to some may appear horrifying and offensive to another group. The modern media are full of reports of one group's activities while the tone and form in which that report is delivered already express an opinion on the part of the person delivering the message. Since the ancient Mesopotamians are already so far removed from us in time and space, to further judge their emotions and approach to their religious practice without their ability to explain does not seem useful for the study or helpful.

Nor does this book provide much comparative discussion. This is not for the lack of numerous places for such comparison nor because points of comparison did not appear to the writer. Again, because we have a limited range of data that focuses on the personal devotion of the individual, making those comparisons could be off base, especially in comparison to modern religions.

Many of the specific examples used to show how elements of ancient Mesopotamian religion developed focus on the role of politics. Because we are examining the religion over a long period of time, this can appear to be blatant manipulation of the system, with those shifts connecting easily to particular events at the time. The same could be true for most religions in existence for a long time, but modern adherents have the advantage of explaining why those shifts are not purely political or do not change the religion fundamentally, if they are even aware of such an evolution. Quite likely the situation for modern religions and their adherents is not dissimilar from ancient Mesopotamia, but again, we do not have the informants to help us understand the situation.

In the modern context adherents may recognize how components of a religion can change without radically modifying their practices in a way that is not acccessible for ancient Mesopotamia. Did imprisoning Marduk and placing Assur's name in the *Enuma Elish* change the way people felt about the New Year festival? If so, did this come about in one day and then everyone forgot? We have no way of knowing, because it is unlikely that the personal reactions to such an event were ever recorded.

127

The absence of the personal element in this study may make it appear as though that was not a component of ancient Mesopotamian religion. Perhaps that is the case. While we know of personal deities, discussed in Chapter 5 on the pantheon, and we have texts of people's pleas and petitions to these deities or a devotee's expression of thanks, we do not know much of how people felt about matters beyond those texts. There is also little about specific individual feelings towards the more major deities, with the exception of the king's relationship to them (see Chapter 10, "Kingship, Religion, and the Gods").

To a large extent, we must rely on other extant texts to reconstruct what we can about ancient Mesopotamian religion. From these, we learn that the Mesopotamians were not focused on the future, making the world better, or what happens to people in some other time, even after death. Most of these documents express an interest in the here and now and, for some, especially kings, being remembered in the future. The point of serving the deity was not to attain some other existence, but to have the best possible life in this world. This is not to say that people did not care at all about the future or about the deities, or that some people did not feel a special devotion for their deities, but simply that this was not the primary focus.

Another problem with trying to understand ancient Mesopotamian religion and how it functioned lies with the accessibility of data. Modern study of ancient Mesopotamia is still fairly young, since our awareness of the ancient Near Eastern world really begins only in the middle of the nineteenth century. That period witnessed the initial developments in archaeology of the region, and it was from then that languages of tablets recovered in those excavations were deciphered, grammars were written, texts translated, published, and interpreted, and the historical outline of the region determined. A great deal of work was accomplished in a short period of time. Only in recent years did access to some of these languages become more accessible through grammars,[1] dictionaries,[2] and publica-

---

1. Von Soden, *Grundriss der akkadischen Grammatik;* Edzard, *Sumerian Grammar;* Huehnergard, *A Grammar of Akkadian.*

2. *Chicago Assyrian Dictionary;* Sjöberg, *Pennsylvania Sumerian Dictionary;* von Soden, *Akkadisches Handwörterbuch;* Parpola and Whiting, *Assyrian-English-Assyrian Dictionary;* and Black, George, and Postgate, *A Concise Dictionary of Akkadian,* to name some of the more widely used in the U.S.

tion of critical editions of the texts. Considering all of this, the field remains somewhat difficult to access for nonspecialists, and many areas that may be of interest to scholars of religion have not yet been thoroughly treated. Thus, not all of the important studies I would like to have consulted are available.

The problem of resources is connected to the issue of finding a middle of the road, as noted in the Introduction. In recent years a number of introductions to the history of Mesopotamia have appeared, so accessing the historical outline of the region is no longer difficult. That cannot be said for other areas of interest with relevance to the topic of religion. For example, as noted in Chapter 2, "Tools for the Study of Ancient Mesopotamian Religion," most of the texts and artifacts upon which our knowledge is based were found in archaeological contexts, both scientifically acquired and less so. Yet despite the importance of understanding the archaeology in order to situate the available artifacts and structures, no recent introduction to the archaeology of Mesopotamia is widely available. Nor are there general or introductory resources on ancient Mesopotamian art — what was produced, how it functioned, and its relevance in the religious context. Extremely important art objects do exist, but the place of Mesopotamia in the field of art history is still rather small, and although some technical studies have been published, the coverage is rather spotty.

Understanding the ancient Mesopotamian pantheon is also difficult because other than a few studies here and there about specific deities, there are not many. For example, there are volumes dedicated to some of the major deities such as Anu, and specialized studies about aspects of Enlil and Inanna/Ishtar, but few comprehensive studies that review all the data following the transformations of one deity through time or even the shape of the pantheon in a particular period. Such studies would be difficult, but would seem quite possible. They would not only help better understand the religion of ancient Mesopotamia but might also benefit other fields such as biblical studies and the study of religion in general by facilitating more and possibly better comparative work.

The scarcity of material on art and the personal element may have made the ancient Mesopotamians or their religion appear cold and removed. That was certainly not the intent. Despite the dearth of direct personal references to religion and its place in the world, a number of instances survive where the ancient Mesopotamians expressed joy in their existence and the world.

While in general female scribes were few in number, two insights, placed in the mouths of female characters, may best sum up a view of the world that could offer insight beyond the ancient world. According to the Epic of Gilgamesh, when Gilgamesh is on his way to learn the secret of immortality from Utnapishtum, before leaving civilization he stops at a tavern. There the alewife tells him that, although the gods set aside death for humankind, he should, among other things, "pay heed to the little one that holds on to thy hand, let thy spouse delight in thy bosom! For this is the task of [mankind]!"[3] As noted in the discussion on mythology, Ereshkigal, the goddess who reigns in the Netherworld, describes her role as eating clay for bread, drinking muddy water for beer, and weeping for young men forced to abandon sweethearts, girls wrenched from their lovers' laps, and for the infant child expelled before its time.[4] Perhaps this is simply sage advice admonishing us, even in our modern world, that we should remember more often to go home, hug our kids, our spouses, eat some good food, and enjoy a nice beer.

3. Epic of Gilgamesh, tablet x column iii lines 10ff.; *ANET*, 90.
4. Descent of Ishtar to the Netherworld, lines 32-36.

Bibliography

Adams, Robert McC. *The Heartland of Cities: Surveys of Ancient Settlement and Land on the Central Floodplain of the Euphrates.* Chicago: University of Chicago Press, 1981.

Aldred, Cyril. *The Egyptians.* Rev. ed. London: Thames and Hudson, 1987.

The American Schools of Oriental Research (ASOR). http://www.asor.org/excavations/policy.html.

Annus, Amar. *The Standard Babylonian Epic of Anzu: Introduction, Cuneiform Text, Transliteration, Score, Glossary, Indices and Sign List.* SAACT 3. Helsinki: Neo-Assyrian Text Corpus Project, University of Helsinki Press, 2001.

Arevalier, Nicole. "The French Scientific Delegation in Persia." In Harper, Aruz, and Tallon, *The Royal City of Susa,* 16-19.

Arnold, Bill T. "What Has Nebuchadnezzar to Do with David: On the Neo-Babylonian Period and Early Israel." In Chavalas and Younger, *Mesopotamia and the Bible,* 330-55.

Assman, Jan. "Monotheism and Polytheism." In Johnston, *Ancient Religions,* 17-31.

Beaulieu, Paul-Alain. *The Reign of Nabonidus, King of Babylon, 556-539 B.C.* YNER 10. New Haven: Yale University Press, 1989.

Beckman, Gary. "How Religion Was Done." In Snell, *A Companion to the Ancient Near East,* 343-53.

Black, Jeremy, and Anthony Green. *Gods, Demons and Symbols of Ancient Mesopotamia: An Illustrated Dictionary.* Austin: University of Texas Press, 1992.

Black, Jeremy, Andrew George, and Nicholas Postgate. *A Concise Dictionary of Akkadian.* Santag 10. Wiesbaden: Harrassowitz, 1999.

Boden, Peggy. "The Mesopotamian Washing of the Mouth [*Mīs Pî*] Ritual." Diss., Johns Hopkins, 1998.

Borger, Rykle. *Assyrisch-babylonische Zeichenliste*. Alter Orient und Altes Testament 33/33a. 4th ed. Germany: Butzon & Bercker Develaer, 1988.

Bottéro, Jean. *Mesopotamia: Writing, Reasoning, and the Gods*. Trans. Zainab Bahrani and Marc Van De Mieroop. Chicago: University of Chicago Press, 1992.

————. *Religion in Ancient Mesopotamia*. Trans. T. L. Fagan. Chicago: University of Chicago Press, 2001.

Brinkman, J. A. *Materials and Studies for Kassite History*. Vol. 1: *A Catalogue of Cuneiform Sources Pertaining to Specific Monarchs of the Kassite Dynasty*. Chicago: Oriental Institute, University of Chicago, 1976.

————. *Prelude to Empire: Babylonian Society and Politics, 747-626 B.C.* Occasional Publications of the Babylonian Fund 7. Philadelphia: University Museum, 1984.

Brisch, Nicole, ed. *Religion and Power: Divine Kingship in the Ancient World and Beyond*. Oriental Institute Seminars 4. Chicago: Oriental Institute, University of Chicago, 2008.

Buccellati, G. "Through a Tablet Darkly: A Reconstruction of Old Akkadian Monuments Described in Old Babylonian Copies." In *The Tablet and the Scroll: Near Eastern Studies in Honor of William W. Hallo*, ed. Mark E. Cohen, Daniel C. Snell, and David B. Weisberg, 58-71. Bethesda: CDL, 1993.

Ceram, C. W. *Gods, Graves, and Scholars: The Story of Archaeology*. Trans. E. B. Garside. New York: Knopf, 1951.

Chavalas, Mark W., ed. *Historical Sources in Translation: The Ancient Near East*. Oxford: Blackwell, 2006.

————, and K. Lawson Younger, Jr., eds. *Mesopotamia and the Bible: Comparative Explorations*. Grand Rapids: Baker, 2002.

Civil, Miguel. "Sumerian." In *OEANE*, 5:92-95.

Clifford, Richard J. *Creation Accounts in the Ancient Near East and the Bible*. CBQMS 26. Washington: Catholic Biblical Association, 1994.

Cogan, Mordechai. "Cyrus Cylinder." In Hallo, *The Context of Scripture* 2:314-16.

Cohen, Mark E. *The Cultic Calendars of the Ancient Near East*. Bethesda: CDL, 1993.

Cole, Steven W. *Nippur in Late Assyrian Times c. 755-612*. SAA Studies 4. Helsinki: Neo-Assyrian Text Corpus Project of the Academy of Finland and the Finnish Oriental Society, 1996.

————, and Peter Machinist. *Letters from Priests to the Kings Esarhaddon and Assurbanipal*. SAA 13. Helsinki: Helsinki University Press, 1998.

Collins, John J. "Cosmology: Time and History." In Johnston, *Ancient Religions*, 59-70.

Cooper, Jerrold S., comp. *The Curse of Agade*. Baltimore: Johns Hopkins University Press, 1983.

————, and Glenn M. Schwartz, eds. *The Study of the Ancient Near East in the 21st*

Century: The William Foxwell Albright Centennial Conference. Winona Lake: Eisenbrauns, 1996.

Dalley, Stephanie, trans. *Myths from Mesopotamia: Creation, the Flood, Gilgamesh, and Others.* Oxford: Oxford University Press, 1989.

Deimel, Anton. *Pantheon babylonicum.* Rome: Sumptibus Pontificii Instituti Biblici, 1914.

Dieulafoy, Jane. "A History of Excavation at Susa: Personalities and Archaeological Methodologies." In Harper, Aruz, and Tallon, *The Royal City of Susa,* 20-24.

Dundes, Alan, ed. *The Flood Myth.* Berkeley: University of California Press, 1988.

Edzard, Dietz Otto. *Sumerian Grammar.* Handbook of Oriental Studies 1/74. Atlanta: Society of Biblical Literature, 2006.

Ellis, Richard S. *Foundation Deposits in Ancient Mesopotamia.* YNER 2. New Haven: Yale University Press, 1968.

Foster, Benjamin R. "Akkadians." In *OEANE,* 1:49-54.

———. *Before the Muses: An Anthology of Akkadian Literature.* 2 vols. Bethesda: CDL, 1993.

———. *From Distant Days: Myths, Tales, and Poetry of Ancient Mesopotamia.* Bethesda: CDL, 1995.

Foxvog, Daniel A. "A Manual of Sacrificial Procedure." In *DUMU-E2-DUB-BA-A: Studies in Honor of Åke W. Sjöberg,* ed. Hermann Behrens, Darlene Loding, and Martha T. Roth, 167-76. Occasional Publications of the Samuel Noah Kramer Fund 11. Philadelphia: University Museum, 1989.

Frayne, Douglas R. *Sargonic and Gutian Period (2334-2113 BC).* The Royal Inscriptions of Mesopotamia, Early Periods 2. Toronto: University of Toronto Press, 1993.

Frymer-Kensky, Tikva. *In the Wake of the Goddesses: Women, Culture, and the Biblical Transformation of Pagan Myth.* New York: Free Press, 1992.

Gates, Marie-Henriette. "Archaeology and the Ancient Near East: Methods and Limits." In Snell, *A Companion to the Ancient Near East,* 63-78.

George, Andrew R. "Babylon Revisited: Archaeology and Philology in Harness." *Antiquity* 67 (1993): 734-46.

———, ed. *House Most High: The Temples of Ancient Mesopotamia.* Mesopotamian Civilizations 5. Winona Lake: Eisenbrauns, 1993.

Gibson, McGuire, and Robert D. Biggs, eds. *The Organization of Power: Aspects of Bureaucracy in the Ancient Near East.* SAOC 46. Chicago: Oriental Institute, University of Chicago, 1987.

Glassner, Jean-Jacques. *Mesopotamian Chronicles.* Ed. Benjamin R. Foster. SBLWAW 19. Atlanta: Society of Biblical Literature, 2004.

Gordon, Cyrus H. *Forgotten Scripts: How They Were Deciphered and Their Impact on Contemporary Culture.* New York: Basic Books, 1968.

Graf, Fritz. "Myth." In Johnston, *Ancient Religions,* 45-58.

Grayson, Albert Kirk. "Assyria and Babylonia." *Or* 49 (1980): 140-94.

————. *Assyrian and Babylonian Chronicles.* TCS 5. Locust Valley: Augustin, 1975.

————. *Assyrian Royal Inscriptions.* Vol. 2: *From Tiglath-Pileser I to Ashur-nasir-apli II.* Wiesbaden: Harrassowitz, 1976.

————. *Assyrian Rulers of the Early First Millennium* BC. Vol. 1: *1114-859* BC. Vol. 2: *858-748* BC. The Royal Inscriptions of Mesopotamia, Assyrian Periods 2-3. Toronto: University of Toronto Press, 1991-96.

————. *Assyrian Rulers of the Third and Second Millennia* BC *(to 1115* BC*).* The Royal Inscriptions of Mesopotamia, Assyrian Periods 1. Toronto: University of Toronto Press, 1987.

Green, Alberto R. W. *The Storm-God in the Ancient Near East.* Biblical and Judaic Studies 8. Winona Lake: Eisenbrauns, 2003.

Hallo, William W., ed. *The Context of Scripture.* Vol. 1: *Canonical Compositions from the Biblical World.* Leiden: Brill, 1997. Vol. 2: *Monumental Inscriptions from the Biblical World,* 2000.

————, and J. J. A. van Dijk, *The Exaltation of Inanna.* YNER 3. New Haven: Yale University Press, 1968.

Harper, Prudence O., Joan Aruz, and Françoise Tallon, eds. *The Royal City of Susa: Ancient Near Eastern Treasures in the Louvre.* New York: Metropolitan Museum of Art, 1992.

Harrak, Amir. *Assyria and Hanigalbat: A Historical Reconstruction of Bilateral Relations from the Middle of the Fourteenth to the End of the Twelfth Centuries* B.C. Texte und Studien zur Orientalistik 4. Hildesheim: Olms, 1987.

Heidel, Alexander. *The Babylonian Genesis: The Story of the Creation.* 2nd ed. Chicago: University of Chicago Press, 1951.

Heimpel, Wolfgang. *Letters to the King of Mari: A New Translation, with Historical Introduction, Notes, and Commentary.* Mesopotamian Civilizations 12. Winona Lake: Eisenbrauns, 2003.

Holloway, Steven W. *Assur Is King! Assur Is King! Religion in the Exercise of Power in the Neo-Assyrian Empire.* Culture and History of the Ancient Near East 10. Leiden: Brill, 2001.

Holm, Tawny L. "Ancient Near Eastern Literature: Genres and Forms." In Snell, *A Companion to the Ancient Near East,* 269-88.

Horowitz, Wayne. *Mesopotamian Cosmic Geography.* Mesopotamian Civilizations 8. Winona Lake: Eisenbrauns, 1998.

Horsnell, Malcolm John Albert. *The Year-Names of the First Dynasty of Babylon.* Vol. 1: *Chronological Matters: The Year-name System and the Date Lists.* Vol. 2: *The Year-Names Reconstructed and Critically Annotated in Light of Their Exemplars.* Canada: McMaster University Press, 1999.

Huehnergard, John. "Akkadian." In *OEANE,* 1:44-49.

————. *A Grammar of Akkadian.* HSS 45. Atlanta: Society of Biblical Literature, 1997.

Huffmon, Herbert B. "A Company of Prophets: Mari, Assyria, Israel." In Nissinen, *Prophecy in Its Ancient Near Eastern Context,* 47-70.

Izre'el, Shlomo. *Adapa and the South Wind: Language Has the Power of Life and Death.* Mesopotamian Civilizations 10. Winona Lake: Eisenbrauns, 2001.

Jacobsen, Thorkild. *The Sumerian King List.* AS 11. Chicago: University of Chicago Press, 1939.

————. *The Treasures of Darkness: A History of Mesopotamian Religion.* New Haven: Yale University Press, 1976.

————, trans. and ed. *The Harps That Once . . . : Sumerian Poetry in Translation.* New Haven: Yale University Press, 1987.

Johnston, Sarah Iles. "Magic." In *Ancient Religions,* 139-52.

————, ed. *Ancient Religions.* Cambridge, Mass.: Belknap Press of Harvard University Press, 2007.

Kilmer, Anne Draffkorn. "The Mesopotamian Concept of Overpopulation and Its Solution as Reflected in the Mythology." *Or* 41 (1972): 160-77.

Klein, Jacob. "Enki and Ninmah." In *Context of Scripture* 1:516-22.

Klengel-Brandt, Evelyn. "Babylonians." Trans. Susan I. Scheidel. In *OEANE,* 1:256-62.

Krebernik, M. "Die Götter-listen aus Faran." *ZA* 76 (1986): 161-204.

Koch-Westenholz, Ulla. *Babylonian Liver Omens: The Chapters Manzāzu, Padānu, and Pān tākalti of the Babylonian Extispicy Series Mainly from Aššurbanipal's Library.* CNI Publications 25. Copenhagen: University of Copenhagen, Museum Tusculanum Press, 2000.

Koldewey, Robert. *Excavations at Babylon.* Trans. A. S. Johns. London: Macmillan, 1914.

Koppen, Frans van. "Old Babylonian Period Inscriptions: Isin-Larsa Period." In Chavalas, *Historical Sources in Translation,* 88-95.

Kramer, S. N. "Inanna's Descent to the Nether World: Continued and Revised." *JCS* 5 (1951): 1-17.

————. "Sumerian Myths and Epic Tales." In *ANET,* 37-59.

————. *The Sumerians: Their History, Culture, and Character.* Chicago: University of Chicago Press, 1963.

————. "The Third Tablet of the Ur Version of 'Inanna's Descent to the Nether World.'" *APSP* 124 (1980): 299-310.

Kuhrt, Amelie. *The Ancient Near East c. 3000-330 B.C.* 2 vols. Routledge History of the Ancient World. London: Routledge, 1995.

Labat, René, and Florence Malbran-Labat. *Manuel d'épigraphie akkadienne: Signes, syllabaire, idéogrammes.* 6th ed. Paris: Geuthner, 1995.

Lambert, W. G. *Babylonian Wisdom Literature.* Oxford: Clarendon, 1960.

————. "DINGIR ŠA.DIB₂.BA Incantations." *JNES* 33 (1974): 267-322.

————. "The Historical Development of the Mesopotamian Pantheon: A Study in

Sophisticated Polytheism." In *Unity and Diversity: Essays in the History, Literature, and Religion of the Ancient Near East,* ed. Hans Goedicke and J. J. M. Roberts, 191-200. Baltimore: Johns Hopkins University Press, 1975.

———. "Myth and Mythmaking in Sumer and Akkad." In *CANE,* 3:1825-35.

———, and A. R. Millard. *Atra-Hasis: The Babylonian Story of the Flood.* Oxford: Clarendon, 1969.

Lapinkivi, Pirjo. *The Sumerian Sacred Marriage: In the Light of Comparative Evidence.* SAA Studies 15. Helsinki: Neo-Assyrian Text Corpus Project, University of Helsinki, 2004.

Larsen, Mogens Trolle. *The Aššur-nādā Archive.* Old Assyrian Archives 1. PIHANS 96. Leiden: Nederlands Instituut voor het nabije Oosten, 2002.

———. "The "Babel/Bible" Controversy and Its Aftermath." In *CANE,* 1:95-106.

———. *The Old Assyrian City-State and Its Colonies.* Mesopotamia 4. Copenhagen: Akademisk, 1976.

Lieberman, Stephen J. "Nippur: City of Decisions." In *Nippur at the Centennial: Papers Read at the 35e Rencontre Assyriologique Internationale, Philadelphia, 1988,* ed. Maria deJong Ellis, 127-36. Occasional Publications of the Samuel Noah Kramer Fund 14. Philadelphia: Babylonian Section, University Museum, 1992.

Lipiński, Edward. *The Aramaeans: Their Ancient History, Culture, Religion.* OLA 100. Leuven: Peeters, 2000.

Litke, Richard L. *A Reconstruction of the Assyro-Babylonian God-Lists AN:dA-num and AN:Anu šá amēli.* Texts from the Babylonian Collection 3. Bethesda: CDL, 1998.

Lloyd, Seton. *The Archaeology of Mesopotamia: From the Old Stone Age to the Persian Conquest.* Rev. ed. London: Thames and Hudson, 1984.

Longman, Tremper, III. "The Adad-guppi Autobiography." In Hallo, *The Context of Scripture* 1.

Luckenbill, Daniel David. *The Annals of Sennacherib.* OIP 2. Chicago: University of Chicago Press, 1924.

Magid, Glen. "Sumerian Early Dynastic Royal Inscriptions."In Chavalas, *Historical Sources in Translation,* 4-16.

Mander, Pietro. *Il Pantheon di Abu-Sālabīkh: contributo all studio del pantheon sumerico arcaico.* Naples: Instituto Universitario Orientale, Dipartamento di Studi Asiatici, 1986.

Margueron, Jean-Claude. "Mari." In *OEANE,* 3:413-17.

McClellan, Thomas L. "12th Century B.C. Syria: Comments on H. Sader's Paper." In Ward and Joukowsky, *The Crisis Years,* 164-73.

Meyers, Eric M., ed. *The Oxford Encyclopedia of Archaeology in the Near East.* 5 vols. Oxford: Oxford University Press, 1997.

Michalowski, Piotr. "Charisma and Control: On Continuity and Change in Early

Mesopotamian Bureaucratic Systems." In Gibson and Biggs, *Organization of Power,* 55-68.

———. "Mortal Kings of Ur: A Short Century of Divine Rule in Ancient Mesopotamia." In Brisch, *Religion and Power,* 33-45.

———. "Sailing to Babylon, Reading the Dark Side of the Moon." In Cooper and Schwartz, *The Study of the Ancient Near East in the 21st Century,* 177-93.

———. "Sumerians." In *OEANE,* 5:95-101.

———, ed. *The Lamentation over the Destruction of Sumer and Ur.* Mesopotamian Civilizations 1. Winona Lake: Eisenbrauns, 1989.

Moran, William L. "Atrahasis: The Babylonian Story of the Flood." *Bib* 52 (1971): 51-61.

———, ed. *The Amarna Letters.* Baltimore: Johns Hopkins University Press, 1992.

Murphy, Roland. "Wisdom in the OT." In *ABD,* 6:920-31.

Muscarella, Oscar White. *The Lie Became Great: The Forgery of Ancient Near Eastern Cultures.* Studies in the Art and Archaeology of Antiquity 1. Groningen: Styx, 2000.

Nemet-Nejat, Karen Rhea. *Daily Life in Ancient Mesopotamia.* Westport: Greenwood, 1998.

Nissen, Hans J. *The Early History of the Ancient Near East 9000-2000 B.C.* Trans. Elizabeth Lutzeier with Kenneth J. Northcott. Chicago: University of Chicago Press, 1988.

Nissinen, Martti, ed. *Prophecy in Its Ancient Near Eastern Context: Mesopotamian, Biblical, and Arabian Perspectives.* SBLSymS 13. Atlanta: Society of Biblical Literature, 2000.

Oates, Joan. *Babylon.* Rev. ed. London: Thames and Hudson, 1986.

Oppenheim, A. Leo. *Ancient Mesopotamia: Portrait of a Dead Civilization.* Rev. ed. by Erica Reiner. Chicago: University of Chicago Press, 1977.

Parpola, Simo. *Assyrian Prophecies.* SAA 9. Helsinki: Helsinki University Press, 1997.

———, and Robert M. Whiting, eds. *Assyrian-English-Assyrian Dictionary.* Helsinki: Neo-Assyrian Text Corpus Project, 2007.

Poebel, Arno. "The Assyrian King List from Khorsabad." *JNES* 1 (1942): 247-306.

Porter, Barbara Nevling. *Images, Power, Politics: Figurative Aspects of Esarhaddon's Babylonian Policy.* Philadelphia: American Philosophical Society, 1993.

Postgate, J. N. *Early Mesopotamia: Society and Economy at the Dawn of History.* London: Routledge, 1992.

Pritchard, James B. *Ancient Near Eastern Texts Relating to the Old Testament.* 3rd ed. Princeton: Princeton University Press, 1969.

Rawlinson, H. E. *The Cuneiform Inscriptions of Western Asia.* Vol. 1: *A Selection from the Historical Inscriptions of Chaldaea, Assyria, and Babylonia.* London: Harrison and Sons, 1861.

Roaf, Michael. "Palaces and Temples in Ancient Mesopotamia." In *CANE*, 1:423-41.

Robertson, John F. "The Social and Economic Organization of Ancient Mesopotamian Temples." In *CANE*, 1:443-54.

Rochberg, Francesca(-Halton). "Astronomy and Calendars in Ancient Mesopotamia." In *CANE*, 3:1925-40.

———. "Calendars. Ancient Near East." In *ABD*, 1:810-14.

Roth, Martha T. *Law Collections from Mesopotamia and Asia Minor.* SBLWAW 6. Atlanta: Scholars, 1995.

Roux, Georges. *Ancient Iraq.* Harmondsworth: Penguin, 1980.

Russell, John Malcolm. *From Nineveh to New York: The Strange Story of the Assyrian Reliefs in the Metropolitan Museum and the Hidden Masterpiece at Canford School.* New Haven: Yale University Press, 1997.

Sader, Helene. "The 12th Century B.C. in Syria: The Problem of the Rise of the Aramaeans." In Ward and Joukowsky, *The Crisis Years*, 157-63.

Sasson, Jack M., ed. *Civilizations of the Ancient Near East.* 4 vols. New York: Scribner's, 1995.

Schneider, Tammi J. *A New Analysis of the Royal Annals of Shalmaneser III.* Ann Arbor: University Microfilms, 1991.

Schwartz, Glenn M. "Pastoral Nomadism in Ancient Western Asia." In *CANE*, 1:249-58.

Selz, Gerhard J. "The Divine Prototypes." In Brisch, *Religion and Power*, 13-31.

Sigrist, René Marcel. *Les sattukku dans l'Èšumeša durant la période d'Isin et Larsa.* Bibliotheca Mesopotamica 11. Malibu: Undena, 1984.

Silverman, David. "Divinity and Deities in Ancient Egypt." In *Religion in Ancient Egypt: Gods, Myths, and Personal Practice*, ed. Byron E. Shafer, 7-87. Ithaca: Cornell University Press, 1991.

Sjoberg, Åke W. "The Old Babylonian Eduba." In *Sumerological Studies in Honor of Thorkild Jacobsen on His Seventieth Birthday, June 7, 1974*, ed. Stephen J. Lieberman, 159-80. AS 20. Chicago: University of Chicago Press, 1975.

———, ed. *The Sumerian Dictionary of the University Museum of the University of Pennsylvania.* Philadelphia: Babylonian Section, University Museum, 1984–.

Smith, George. *The Chaldaean Account of Genesis.* London: Low, Manstan, Seare, and Rivington, 1876.

———. "The Chaldean Account of the Deluge." In Dundes, *The Flood Myth*, 29-48.

Smith, Jonathan Z. "Religion, Religions, Religious." In *Critical Terms for Religious Studies*, ed. Mark C. Taylor, 269-84. Chicago: University of Chicago Press, 1998.

Snell, Daniel C. "The Historian's Task." In *A Companion to the Ancient Near East*, 95-108.

————, ed. *A Companion to the Ancient Near East*. Blackwell Companions to the Ancient World. Malden: Blackwell, 2007.

Soden, Wolfram von. *Akkadisches Handwörterbuch*. 3 vols. Wiesbaden: Harrassowitz, 1965-81.

————. *Grundriss der akkadischen Grammatik*. AnOr 47. 2nd ed. Rome: 1969.

Starr, Ivan, ed. *Queries to the Sungod: Divination and Politics in Sargonid Assyria*. SAA 4. Helsinki: Helsinki University Press, 1990.

Steinkeller, Piotr. "Administrative and Economic Organization of the Ur III State: The Core and the Periphery." In Gibson and Biggs, *The Organization of Power*, 19-41.

Stone, Elizabeth. "The Social Role of the Naditu Woman in Old Babylonian Nippur." *JESHO* 25 (1982): 50-70.

Tadmor, Hayim. *The Inscriptions of Tiglath-Pileser III, King of Assyria: Critical Edition, with Introductions, Translations, and Commentary*. Jerusalem: Israel Academy of Sciences and Humanities, 1994.

Tallqvist, Knut. *Akkadische Götterepitheta*. Helsinki: Societas orientalis fennica, 1938.

Talon, Philippe. *The Standard Babylonian Creation Myth: Enuma Elis*. SAACT 4. Helsinki: Helsinki University Press, 2005.

Thureau-Dangin, F. "L'inscription des lions de Til-Barsib." *RA* 27 (1930): 1-21.

Toorn, Karel van der. "Mesopotamian Prophecy between Immanence and Transcendence: A Comparison of Old Babylonian and Neo-Assyrian Prophecy." In Nissinen, *Prophecy in Its Ancient Near Eastern Context*, 71-87.

Van de Mieroop, Marc. *The Ancient Mesopotamian City*. Oxford: Clarendon, 1997.

————. *A History of the Ancient Near East ca. 3000-323*. 2nd ed. Malden: Blackwell, 2007.

Vanstiphout, H. L. J. "Disputations." In *The Context of Scripture* 1:575-93.

Villard, Pierre. "Shamshi-Adad and Sons: The Rise and Fall of an Upper Mesopotamian Empire." In *CANE*, 2:873-83.

Walker, Christopher, and Michael Dick. *The Induction of the Cult Image in Ancient Mesopotamia: The Mesopotamian Mis Pi Ritual*. SAA Literary Texts 1. Helsinki: Neo-Assyrian Corpus Project, 2001.

Ward, William A., and Martha Sharp Joukowsky, eds. *The Crisis Years: The 12th Century, From Beyond the Danube to the Tigris*. Dubuque: Kendall/Hunt, 1989.

Weiss, Harvey. "Akkade." In *OEANE*, 1:41-44.

Westenholz, Joan Goodnick. *Legends of the Kings of Akkade: The Texts*. Mesopotamia Civilizations 7. Winona Lake: Eisenbrauns, 1997.

Wiggermann, F. A. M. "Theologies, Priests, and Worship in Ancient Mesopotamia." In *CANE*, 1857-70.

Wilhelm, Gernot. *The Hurrians*. Trans. Jennifer Barnes. Warminster: Aris and Philips, 1989.

Winter, Irene. "Opening the Eyes and Opening the Mouth: The Utility of Comparing Images in Worship in India and Ancient Near East." In *Ethnography and Personhood: Notes from the Field,* ed. Michael W. Meister, 129-62. Jaipur: Rawat, 2000.

————. "Touched by the Gods: Visual Evidence for the Divine Status of Rulers in the Ancient Near East." In Brisch, *Religion and Power,* 73-98.

Wohlstein, Herman. *The Sky-God An-Anu: Head of the Mesopotamian Pantheon in Sumerian-Akkadian Literature.* Trans. Salvator Attanasio. Jericho, NY: Stroock, 1976.

Yee, Gale A. *Poor Banished Children of Eve: Woman as Evil in the Hebrew Bible.* Minneapolis: Fortress, 2003.

Zettler, Richard L. "Adminstration of the Temple of Inanna at Nippur under the Third Dynasty of Ur: Archaeological and Documentary Evidence." In Gibson and Biggs, *The Organization of Power,* 117-31.

————. "Written Documents as Excavated Artifacts and the Holistic Interpretation of the Mesopotamian Archaeological Record." In Cooper and Schwartz, *The Study of the Ancient Near East in the 21st Century,* 81-101.

Time Line for Ancient Mesopotamia

Early Periods

Halaf	6100-5400
Ubaid	5300-3800
Uruk	4100-2900
Jemdet Nasr	3100-2900
Early Dynastic I	2900-2800
Early Dynastic II	2800-2600
Early Dynastic III	2600-2334 (Rise of Sargon)

Akkad

Sargon	2334-2279
Rimush	2278-2270
Mainshtushu	2269-2255
Naram-Sin	2254-2218
Sharkalisharri	2217-2193

Creating a precise chronology for the ancient Near East, and even just the Mesopo-tamian part of it, is a complicated process. Most introductions to the history of the an-cient Near East will discuss the complex issues involved in trying to tie all the various indicators together to come to something that works for all areas at all times. Despite that, having a basic outline available is helpful to place events. As a result, this time line generally follows the middle chronology and is in no way authoritative but provided for students to better understand the relationship over time of the various players with each other. Note that all dates are B.C.E.

Period of Confusion 2192-2190

Ur III

Ur Namma	2112-2095
Shulgi	2094-2047
Amar-Sin	2046-2038
Shu-Sin	2037-2029
Ibbi-Sin	2028-2004

Isin/Larsa Period 2017-1835

Ishbi-Irra	2017-1985

Old Babylonian		**Assyrian**		**Mari**	
		Shamshi-Adad	1813-1781		
		Ishme-Dagan	1780-?	Yasmah-Addu	1795-76
Hammurabi	1792-1750			Zimri-Lim	1775-1762
Samsuiluna	1749-1712				
Abi-eshhuh	1711-1684				
Ammiditana	1683-1647				
Ammisaduqa	1646-1626				
Samsuditana	1625-1595				

Kassite Babylonia		**Assyria**	
Agum II	1602-1585		
Brunaburiash II	1380-1350	Assur-uballit I	1363-1328
		Shalmaneser I	1273-1244
		Tukulti-Ninurta I	1243-1207
Khashtiliash IV	1232-1225		

Babylonia		Assyria	
Nebuchadnezzar I	1124-1103	Tiglath-Pileser I	1114-1076
		Adad-Nirari II	911-891
		Assurnasirpal II	883-859
Nabu-apla-iddina	885-828	Shalmaneser III	858-824
		Shamshi-Adad IV	823-811
		Tiglath-Pileser III	744-727
		Shalmaneser V	726-722
		Sargon II	721-705
		Sennacherib	704-681
		Esarhaddon	668-627
		Assurbanipal	668-627
Nabopolassar	626-605	Assyria overthrown by 609	
Nebuchadnezzar II	604-562		
Evil-Merodach	561-560		
Neriglissar	559-556		
Labashi-Marduk	556		
Nabonidus	555-539		

Index